DR. B.R. AMBEDKAR AND THE DYNAMICS OF NEO-BUDDHISM

DR. B.R. AMBEDKAR AND THE DYNAMICS OF NEO-BUDDHISM

Rev Dr K DAVID PANDYAN, Ph D, B D

GYAN

Published by

GYAN

Gyan Publishing House
5, Ansari Road
Daryaganj, New Delhi-110002
Phone: 011-47034999, 9811692060
E-mail: books@gyanbooks.com

Distribution Network
gyanbooks.com
India, USA, Canada, UK, Australia, France

ISBN: 978-81-212-0508-5 (HB)

Reprint in India, 2024
First Published, 1996

Printed at: Gyan Press, Delhi.

Dr. B.R. Ambedkar and the Dynamics of Neo-Buddhism
Author: Rev. Dr K. David Pandyan

Dedication

To my friend and unique source of inspiration

Dr. KENNETH J. THOMAS Ph.D.,

Consultant, Asia-Pacific Region

The United Bible Societies, New York, USA.

PREFACE

The genesis of my interest in 'Neo-Buddhism' goes way back to late 1978. My first encounter with a Neo-Buddhist was by chance; but that encounter left an indelible mark in my mind; it finally led to my sustained interest in the Neo-Buddhist movement. I believe that this book will not be the end of my scholastic and research pursuits in this direction.

I owe my gratitude to many people for making this research possible. First and foremost, I would thank Dr. S.P. Dubey for his constant guidance. Mere words cannot adequately express my gratitude to him. He had become my friend, philosopher and guide, I shall remain grateful to him always. I must also express my gratitude to his wife Mrs. K. Dubey for her hospitality during my discussions with Prof. Dubey.

I am grateful to the friends of mine at Nagpur, who had helped me during my research endeavours, namely, Prof. M.K. Dongre; Mr. Khandekar; Prof. Kavade; Mr. Valvekar and Mr. Manavkar. I also would like to express my gratitude to Revd. M.A. Daniel for providing me accommodation when I was conducting Field Research at Nagpur.

My gratitude is also due to Dr. J.P. Shukla, Vice-Chancellor of Rani Durgavati University, Jabalpur; Revd. Dr. G.R. Singh, (Principal), Mr. H. Hamilton (Librarian), Revd. Rodgers, Revd. F.J. Valsalen, Revd. Daniel George (Professors) and Mrs. & Mr. I.G. Tayade of Leonard Theological College, Jabalpur. Revd. Dr. D.C. Scott, former Professor of Religions, Leonard Theological College, Jabalpur needs special mention, for it was he who sparked off this research and helped me to draft the questionnaire for field research. I must thank Prof. Mourya of Ambedkar Research Institute, Indore for his help while at Indore. My gratitude is also due to Revd. Dr. Satish C. Gyan, former Professor of Religion at Leonard Theological College and at present Director, RCDRC (Raipur Church's Development and Relief Committee), Raipur for all his help.

I will be failing in my duty, if I do not express my gratitude to my wife Mrs. Kanaklata Pandyan, who always remained the prime source of inspiration. I know the sacrifices she had made to make me what I am today. I thank my daughter Miss Pearl Rajkumari for her help and care when I was at work. I thank Mrs. C. Scott and Mrs. A. Babu for helping me with typing.

I am very grateful to M/s. Gyan Publishing House, New Delhi, specially Mr. B.P. Garg, its Chief Executive—for bringing out this book.

Rev Dr K DAVID PANDYAN

Pachmarhi, M.P.

PROLOGUE

While I was a student at Leonard Theological College, Jabalpur, our class was sent to Nagpur for fifteen days to fulfil a course requirement. This was in November 1978 and our assignment involved studying the problems of rickshaw pullers. In this connection, I happened to visit the home of a rickshaw puller—Shri Shinde was his name—who dwelt in a slum area like most of the rickshaw pullers do. But as I stepped into the area surrounding his house, I was surprised to see a decently built hut with cement flooring and a septic tank attached. Though the roof was covered with palm leaves, the 'house' was electrified. During the course of our conversation, I came to know that (i) the 'house' was his own; (ii) his wife supplemented to the income of the family by tailoring and owned a sewing machine; (iii) his eldest son was a final year student of an engineering college; (iv) his younger son also was planning to study engineering; (v) while his daughter was given away in marriage, his niece was a student of the Medical college. He confessed that he was illiterate and belonged to the Scheduled Caste (Mahar); he had given up his ancestral menial job and instead opted to pull rickshaw for his livelihood. I asked him how he managed to achieve all these. In reply he pointed his index finger upward toward a photoframe fixed above the doorway and declared that the two men in the photopicture inside the frame were responsible for what he had achieved. In that photoframe were two photopictures juxtaposed—the Buddha's and Dr. Ambedkar's. He further told me that he had embraced Buddhism in 1956 along with Dr. B.R. Ambedkar.

I had known that Buddhism had originated in India, but had become almost extinct in the land of its origin though it flourished in neighbouring countries like Ceylon (now Sri Lanka) and Burma. (now Myanmar) I had learnt later that Buddhism was revived in certain pockets of Maharashtra; the revived sect of Buddhism came to be called 'Neo-Buddhism', the leader of this revival was Dr. B.R. Ambedkar, the 'father of Indian Constitution'. Now I had come across a Neo-Buddhist face to face, who was one of the 5,00,000 of mass converts to Buddhism in November 1956. This was the beginning of my interest in the study of Neo-Buddhism. For no specific reason, during the next few days of my study at Nagpur, during free time, I visited frequently *Dikshabhoomi* (the venue of the 1956 mass conversion), and also met many second generation educated Neo-Buddhists, who were small or young when their parents embraced Buddhism in 1956 along with Dr. B.R. Ambedkar, and also met Buddhist monks, the foremost of whom was late Badanta Anand Kausalyayan—a Brahmin turned Buddhist monk, and a scholar of repute.

The following summer, with a desire to write a monograph on Neo-Buddhism, I spent quite a few days at Nagpur. I had prepared a questionnaire for a positive study of Neo-Buddhist movement (enclosed in the appendix). My findings then and the subsequent readings on Neo-Buddhism prompted me to rationalize the impact and contribution of Dr. B.R. Ambedkar in alleviating the miseries of the Mahars by showing them the path of the Buddha. When I visited *Dikshabhoomi* on 14th April, 1979 (Dr. Ambedkar's 88th birth anniversary), I could see for myself the reverence which the Neo-Buddhists had for the master. Since then, I have been in constant touch with the Neo-Buddhist movement, participating in their meetings and forums. I have visited select Neo-Buddhist pockets in Maharashtra and had the pleasure of interviewing many Neo-Buddhists —literate and illiterate from all walks of life. During the endeavour, I was excited to note that the theories of the two eminent European sociologists, Emile Durkheim of France and Max Weber of Germany and the American Economist Ralph Baldwin agreed with regard to Neo-Buddhism, in its socio-religious contexts. Then I decided to make a detailed study of this movement and this decision resulted in my doctorate and eventually, this book.

CONTENTS

1

INTRODUCTION

THE NEED TO STUDY THE RISE AND FALL OF TRADITIONAL BUDDHISM

In our examination of 'the Dynamics of Neo-Buddhism' in its social and religious contexts, it would be advantageous to be acquainted with (i) the circumstances in which Prince Siddhartha came to be known as the Buddha; and (ii) the rise and fall of Buddhism. We would note that the founder of traditional Buddhism, Gautama the Buddha sought to know the solution to the problem of suffering in the context of his environment; so also the founder of Neo-Buddhism—Dr. B.R. Ambedkar—sought to solve the problem of 'suffering' in the context of his environment. We would note that to seek knowledge, the pursuits of both these great men have been quite different, but perseverance and determination were more or less the same as was their self-disciplining; we would also note that the Buddha left his wife and child in quest of knowledge to find the root of the problem. It is traditionally believed that the Buddha left his sleeping wife and took to asceticism.

Dr. Ambedkar wrote in his *Buddha And His Dhamma,* that he took leave of his approving wife before taking to asceticism *(Parivrajaksa).*

In the 6th century B.C., if Prince Siddhartha, as an ascetic, travelled all the way from Kapilavastu (almost at the foot of the Himalayas in Nepal) to Bodhgaya (in Bihar) and attained enlightenment. In comparison Dr. B.R. Ambedkar travelled overseas to acquire knowledge, with which he could come out with his thoughts. Another aspect of a situation which both men confronted was the social oppression. They sought to alleviate the miseries of the suffering mass of their times showing them a new path in different connotations—but it was the same path. Both these great men proclaimed that 'Salvation' is *here and now* and wrote off such a possibility in the world to come. We would finally note that the Buddhism taught by the original founder of Buddhism, took different shapes like Hinayana, Mahayana, Tantrayana and so also took its very latest development and shape in India in *Navayana* or *Neo-Buddhism.* With these observations to begin with, we would launch into a socio-religious study of *The Dynamics of Neo-Buddhism.*

TRADITIONAL BUDDHISM: ITS RISE AND FALL

1. Gautama, the Buddha and His Quest

Buddhism, a religion of Indian origin, is recognised as one of the major religions of the world and every Indian should legitimately be proud of this phenomenon. When one looks back to visualize what the spiritual and social set up of India was like in the sixth century before Christ, one would note that this was a time when there were many princely states spread all over India and when social and religious systems within the Hindu tradition were firmly established. The *varna* system had taken deep roots in the society at large. The Brahmins, constituting the upper most strata of the Hindu society were the most privileged class.

Their word, more or less, was law and even the kings were dependent on their advice. Proper sacrifices had to be done by kings and citizens through the Brahmins. Sacrifices had become the *Summum Bonum* of life. They had taken so important a place and so cumbersome in day-to-day living of the people, that it appears that to live then was nothing but to perform sacrifices. It was at this time that a young prince renounced his luxury, home and dear ones to find answers to a few puzzling facts of life. He was Siddhartha Gautama, born sometime past the middle of the 6th century B.C. Though it generally agreed that Buddha's birth was around the 6th century B.C. Prof. G.C. Pande says that the Buddha was born in 563 B.C.[1]

It is not out of place to note that the French scholar Emile Senart accepts the actual existence of *A Buddha*, but denies emphatically and vehemently the existence of *ThatBuddha* of whom all know to be *The Buddha*.[2] He is an odd-man-out, for, the rest of the scholars accept the historicity of Gautama, the Buddha as the founder of Buddhism.

There are many myths associated with Buddha's birth which cannot be simply brushed aside, for these legends constitute, the basis of faith for millions of Buddhists all over the world. Even Dr. B.R. Ambedkar, the proponent of Neo-Buddhism, cites the supernatural element regarding the Buddha in his *Buddha And His Dhamma* (I-1-2-8-25).

There are scores of books on the life of one of the greatest men ever lived on earth—Lord Buddha— and any more treatise on his life and mission will be only adding a core to the castle! Such an attempt is beyond our scope. However, it is important for us to note that he was a non-Brahmin of blue blood and that he rebelled against the 'tyranny' of sacrifices and repudiated the self-affliction and mortification for salvation. Another important aspect that we should note is that the traditional belief that he was brought up devoid of any knowledge of suffering. That his chance encounter with an old man, a sick man, a sage and the sight of a corpse had a traumatic effect on his personal life that he left his palace and family to become an ascetic, was strongly repudiated by Dr. B.R. Ambedkar who said: "This answer is absurd on the face of it".[3] Another fact we must note is what Oldenberg points out that "the Buddhists have not attributed Vedic scholarship to their master".[4] But it is conceded that the Buddha had profound knowledge of the Vedas, Vedic religion and the Vedic cult. Ven. Nandasara answers how, "He (Siddharth) went to the professors of knowledge to find out what they did know".[5] Obviously during his talks with knowledgeable persons of his times, he must have made inquiries for which they must have answered from the Vedic point of view and these answers might have helped evolve a system of his own; in the course of such discussions with scholars of orthodox systems, he was gradually building up a heterodox system of his own; the failure of orthodoxy and rituals to drive home to Buddha the meaning and answers to the problems of life must have forced him to try all possible ways and means to attain ultimate knowledge which included severest ascetic discipline and bodily tortures until the day he was *enlightened*. That great day marked a turning point in the history of religions in India and the world at large. As Prof. Pande puts it; "through the practice of *Jnana*, the Buddha obtained enlightenment which consisted of the intuitive knowledge of reality".[6] Thus Siddhartha Gautama came to be known thereafter as the Buddha (the enlightened one). Edward Thomas reproduces the enlightenment scene of the Buddha thus: "(He) Then went in the direction of the Bodhi tree. On the way a grass cutter gave him eight handfuls of grass for the seat. He sat down facing the east with the words, 'may skin, sinew and bone dry up as it will, my flesh and blood grow dry in my body; but without attaining complete enlightenment I will not leave this seat'. ....without his mind being overcome by painful feeling he practised stoppage of breathing until the gods thought he was dead; he took less less and less food until he was reduced to a skeleton....."[7]

In comparison, Dr. Ambedkar's assertion that 'knowledge is power' made him work eighteen hours a day, both at College and Library while in England. As he could not afford lunch, he is said to have saved two slices of bread from his breakfast for his lunch—a sort of seeker of knowledge in the 20th century context!

2. The Buddha's Enlightenment and His Ministry

Consequent to the event of the Buddha's enlightenment, casteism and ritualism were repudiated by the Buddha. D.C. Ahir says: "Prior to the advent of the Buddha, India was unaware of the ethics of equality and universal brotherhood. According to *Purusha sukta* of the *Rig Veda,* the Brahmins came from the mouth of the Brahma, the creator. The Kshatriyas were from the arms; the Vaishyas from the thighs and the Sudras were from the feet. Thus society based on mythical origins was known as the Chaturvarna and was reflected by the principle of graded inequality... This rule of graded inequality regulated their rights and privileges as well... The Buddha revolted against such oppressive social laws and condemned caste system. He challenged the divine origin of the caste and showed the hollowness of the claims of the Brahmins of having been born from the mouth of the Brahma. He also refuted the Brahminic claim that they alone could attain spiritual knowledge and asserted that a man of any caste, colour or creed can develop in his heart such virtues..."[8]

Thus, we find that Buddhism was human dignity oriented, based on equality of all as against the basic Hindu tenets of discrimination of men and women castewise. The Buddha went about preaching this philosophy of equality and propagating his path to reach salvation, i.e. cessation from the law of karma and transmigration—often technically called metamorphosis. The Buddha denounced casteism like this: "One does not become a Brahmana by birth; one does not become an outcaste by birth: One becomes a *Brahmana* by act, one becomes an outcaste by act".[9] The Buddha also abhored violence in any form—animals being sacrificed or men being killed in war—he vehemently condemned. Another great contribution of the Buddha was his attitude towards women regarding which Dr. B.R. Ambedkar in his short work *The Rise and Fall of Hindu Woman* painstakingly drives home as to how the elevated the position of womanhood was downgraded during Brahmanic days and how Buddhism restored parity.[10]

In nutshell the Buddha's message was to :

(i) replace religious orthodoxy, rituals, etc., by a new way which he called Middle Way—neither supernatural nor self-torture to obtain salvation; (ii) propagate universal brotherhood, thus destroy casteism; (iii) educate people that the four Noble Truths and eight-fold path would suffice for the purpose of living and salvation, Nirvana or Nibhana from metamorphosis.

The Buddha had many converts—many from amongst the Brahmins and much more from the lower and lowest castes. Buddhism grew quite fast. Gautama the Buddha lived for quite a ripe age, travelling and teaching. He passed away (Mahaparinirvana) while he was nearing eightieth year at Kushinara sometime in 483-482 B.C. Tradition attributes that the Buddha survived a few attempts on his life by King Ajatasatru and Monk Devadatta.[11]

Another notable aspect that is usually bye-passed is the Buddha's choice of Kushinara as his venue of death, when he realised that his death was imminent. Of the many narratives, Edwards' description of the point that we wish to drive home is most crisp: "... After the meal with Kunda, the Buddha moved on a little way to the Malla town of Kushinara. It is only there that Ananda (the Buddha's close disciple) seems to have realised that the Buddha would die far away from the arena of his life's work. 'Let not the exalted one die in this shanty town, in this town in the middle of the jungle... For Lord there are other great cities such as Champa, Rajagriha, Shravasti, Saketa, Kaushambi and Varanasi. Let the exalted one die in one of them. In these cities are many rich men, princes and heads of houses, believers in the Buddha, who will pay due honour to the remains of the Buddha'. The compilers of the narrative of the last journey shared Ananda's surprise and distate at the impropriety of the Buddha dying in a remote and unsophisticated township, the distaste of the metropolitan to the provincial... The Buddha had to die among barbarians, the unenlightened, in a grove on a simple couch between two flowering trees alone except for Ananda and a few interested by-standers... But there is no reason to doubt that the Buddha knew what he was doing..."[12] What is implied in this, for us to note here, is not that the Buddha chose to die in a small and insignificant town, but that he showed his solidarity with the lowest of the low—the barbarians. This total identity of the Buddha with the lowliest of the strata then, was probably the most important factor to attract Dr. Ambedkar, an enlightened personality of the 20th century and born as an outcaste, into Buddhism, and along with him lakhs of outcastes adopted Buddhism in 1956. This factor is the most emphatic facet of this work.

The exact date of the Buddha's death is not sure as is his date of birth. Saunders, who could place the date of birth to be around 560 B.C., points out diversities relating to his death and says, "the whole question (Buddha's death) has since been thoroughly discussed, notably by Dr. J.F Fleet, who places the death of Gautama on October 13, 482 B.C.".[13] However, the Buddhist Society of India holds the Buddha's birth to be of 563 B.C., Enlightenment 528 B.C. and Mahaparinirvana 483 B.C.[14]

3. Rise and Fall of Buddhism in India

Scholars usually agree that there is ample evidence to suggest that Buddhism was very popular even during the lifetime of the Buddha himself. The Buddha initiated the *Dhamma Chakra Pavattana* (setting the wheel of the *Dhamma* in motion) at Saranath by reasoning with five learned Brahmin seekers and these five became his first batch of disciples. Subsequently, there were many Brahmins and non-Brahmins who became his followers and they took to propagating Buddhism far and near. The Buddha, in course of time, organised two orders: (i) the Order of the Monks; and (ii) the Order of the Laity. Prof. Pande points out that "among the lay disciples important role was played by the moneyed and ruling class. Women too figured prominently as nuns and lay devotees. The religious pretensions of the Brahmins were attacked but the opposition was ideological and sectarian, not social. Many Brahmins joined the new order and there were followers from the lower class too. The Sangha or the Order of Monks was indifferent to caste and all could join on footing of equality, except for Government servants, debtors, slaves, and certain kinds of proclaimed criminals, offenders and those suffering from physical defects. These could not become monks".[15]

The rise of Buddhism appears to have been an answer to unsatiated intellectuals, seeking after the truth. For ordinary people it was an answer to the demands of sacrifices—too expensive and too cumbersome, but inevitable. Women too found a place for themselves in Buddhism which was denied to them hitherto, for that matter their position was non-entity except for being food cooking and baby making machines. The spread of Buddhism began in the kingdoms of Kosala and Magadha.[16]

It is not our purpose here to trace the development of Buddhism, but it is to point out that Buddhism was a revolt against Brahmin orthodoxy. Hence it is rightly called Heterodox. Buddhism became a strong movement. With the conversion of Mauriyan emperor Ashoka (about 270 B.C.) Buddhism became international religion. Prof. Ahmed Shaw says that "this conversion was the turning point of the rise and expansion of Buddhism..."[17] Very true, Emperor Ashoka's conversion into Buddhism created history in the history of religions itself. What probably could have been termed 'yet another religion' became a great religion, breaking the barriers of region and nation and uniting people of all kinds all over the world. That it took various forms in various countries (to the needs of the situations) is a study by itself.

Each of the Buddhist traditions in various forms (*Hinayana, Mahayana,* etc.) had developed its own doctrines building on the seemingly simple *Pancha Sila* and *Ashtanga Marga,* and so also the canonical literature of each form.

The Buddhist presentation of the Middle Way is of syllogistic kind. Thesis, anti-thesis and synthesis: Extreme pleasures—no; Extreme self-mortification—no; Moderation—yes, this could be deemed as the Buddhist Philosophy as a whole. But was this simple philosophy of life easily arrived at by the Buddha? The answer would be an emphatic 'no'. The Buddha had mastered the metaphysical overtones underlying the principles of existence. In an article H.L.N. Sastri writes: "The method of the Buddha is to split up phenomena, to resolve the processes into single constituents and to carry on the analysis until ultimate, subtle and essential elements of existence are reached. ...We have the classification of all elements into mind and matter for which the Buddhists use the words *Nama* and *Rupa*....Buddhist Philosophy is thus an analysis of separate elements or forces which unite in the production of one stream *(santana)* of events....Buddha discovered the elements of existence, their causal connection and the method of suppressing their resistance forever".[18]

Indian metaphysics is rather vast and difficult to comprehend. The Buddha, as a seeker of truth, learnt all and saw all that was around and reduced the heavily loaded complex philosophies then in vogue to a simple and comprehendable *Dhamma*. For a layman simple faith and a guiding principle of ethics would do. That the Buddha did. For the intellectual there was enough to feast. Prof. Sastri states that the Buddha taught people the sustaining cause of life's course and what delivers from life's woes.[19] We may add that the Buddha thus made the puzzling philosophies plain; he found ritualistic sacrifices redundant, and in his system severed; Ethics, he extolled; Equality of all, he emphasised; Thus we find that Buddhism became a boon.

The problem arose only after Buddha's demise. The sayings of the Buddha were collected and compiled. As we know there were four Buddhist councils held, in which seemingly minor issues were dealt with, with utmost sincerity and scruples. Bhikkus' commitments were checked; even Ananda, the Buddha's favourite disciple, was grilled. The Tripitakas, namely—*Vinaya Pitaka* (5 books of Discipline), *Sutta Pitaka* (5 collections popular discourses) and *Abhidhamma Pitaka* (7 books of Philosophy) came into being. But, we find that Buddhism grew by leaps and bounds and flourished. Emperors Ashoka and Kanishka patronised Buddhism and so did the succeeding kings. Great Buddhist philosophers like Nagarjuna and Dhammakirti gave India pride of place.

The advent of Buddhism and the subsequent royal patronage, brought in a new phenomena—the Buddhist art. Royal edicts and inscriptions have become parts of even modern India. The Lion capital and the Dhamma chakra have become our national symbols today. Following persecutions and foreign invasions, Buddhism vanished from the Indian soil, leaving just scars of its glorious past. But, the only religion which had covered almost every nook and corner of the present India, Pakistan and Bangladesh, apart from Hinduism, was Buddhism and had gone beyond the coasts and land of India and went to become the state religion of some of the Asian countries. This is a short account of the Traditional Buddhism over the two milleniums of its existence.

A religion is both for the common people and its clergy. When the Buddha preached and showed people a new way, it was just a way he showed and that too to common people. When the people from all walks of life became the disciples of the Buddha, most of them became Bhikkus; but the householders and businessmen remained in their respective professions. After the demise of the Buddha the monks took to intellectual pursuits or, as we see, were involved in internal bickerings; some accusing the other on silly issues like "carrying salt in a horn. This practice is contrary to Pacittiya 38 which prohibits the storage of food" or "taking meals when the shadow is two fingers broad. This is against Pacittiya which prohibits taking food after midday" or "drinking of buttermilk after meals. This practice is in contravention of Pacittiya 35 which prohibits overeating"[20]... Secondly, as Ambedkar points out, while there was initiation ceremony for Bhikkus, there was none as such for *upasakas*. Thus there was no binding which could have brought in for the feeling a fraternity. Thirdly, as the late Ven. Bhadant Anand Kausalyayan says there were many despicable practices crept into Buddhism which degenerated the values emphasised in Buddhism.[21] All these points were due to the fact that in a Bhikku-dominated Buddhism especially when Mahayana dominated, the laity were ultimately led to believe in *Tantrayana* and subsequently into moral degradations. There was nothing of the old Buddhist colour of purity, virtue and righteousness. During the persecution times, the monks fled further and further towards east and the laity were left without clergy; nor was any single literature which could bind the Buddhist laity together. The *viharas* were destroyed during invasions. What traditional Buddhism needed was to keep and to hold its flock, but how it could have, when its shepherds themselves were fleeing? Some of the Vajrayana scholars (Mahayana's later forms) lived in jungles, alone and away, naked and drinking wine using skull as cups.[22]

The respect that Buddhism commanded from its inception in the 5th century B.C. till persecution after 5th century A.D. gradually deteriorated and became an object of mockery. The monks alone are to be held guilty of this for they do not appear to have identified themselves with the laymen totally and hence there was no proper communication. It is obvious that whatever glory Buddhism enjoyed was mainly due to Buddhist kings like Ashoka, who personally took interest in the spread of the religion by making Buddhism a state Religion. When the ruling king was disinterested the state of the religion was in bad shape. The Bhikkus seem to have been on the quest of scholastic excellence or experimenting on new trends and new forms. Buddhist literature was increasing but that could be understood only by the scholars who were primarily monks. It is not known how many laity had access to Buddhist literature, leave alone Buddhist canonical literature.

If the emergence of Buddhism was at the expense of Brahminical cult and ritualistic sacrifices, the resurgence of Brahminism was due only to the lethargy and laxity of the monks. Ahir quotes Cunningham, the great archaeologist who explored and excavated Kushinagara: "Buddhism had in fact become an old and wornout creed, whose mendicant monks no longer begged their food, but was supported by land, long since appropriated to the monasteries. The *Sramanas* and *Bhikus* were not like those of ancient days, the learned and the wise, whose bodily abstinance and contemplative devotion combined with practical exhortations and holy example excited the pious wonder of the people. The modern Buddhists had relapsed into an unadolent and corrupt body who were content to spend passive existence in the monotonous routine of monastic life.... there were still some outward signs of religion; but there was no fervent enthusiasm in the lifeless performance of such monotonous routine and the ardent zeal which once burned in the heart of every Buddhist monk for the propagation of his religion had long since had become extinct".[23]

The Buddhist literature was so vast, and no organised laity, no committed monk, as against, persecution on the community, social ostracism, revival of Brahminism. This was the situation which the vast majority of the Buddhist laity had to face.

Yet another factor that affected the standing of traditional Buddhism specially from the second century A.D. onwards was the deification of the Buddha as a Bodhisattva in the Mahayana School that he would come again and again to save mankind. This thought was similar to the Hindu concept of *avatara*. Thus the Buddha was not only venerated but also worshipped by all as an *avatara* and gradually Buddhism lost its initial identity as a unique and separate cult. Some of the Buddhist festivals were absorbed into Hinduism and hence Buddhism and Hinduism became like two names of the same religion. In course of time, without an organised shepherding, the minority Buddhists joined the mainstream of their friendly Hindus. They should have done this casually, because Indians by and large are very religious. What might have started as casual, must have become a habit and ultimately part of the system over the generations that succeeded.

In addition to all these events which hastened the fall of Buddhism in India, was the development of Indian philosophy to its highest pinnacle, specially with the emergence of 1. *Dvaita,* 2. *Advaita and* 3. *Visistadvaita*, which were fascinating. Sankara is said to have 'struck terror to the Buddhists'. To counter the brilliance of philosophers like Sankaracharya, there was no Buddhist theologian near nor far.

There was yet another sad situation. One understands if foreign invaders desecrated temples like Somnath or destroy Buddhist shrines like Kot Kangra, but there is evidence that many stupas were brought down by Hindus for materials like bricks for either laying roads, or for making houses. Ahir quotes many such incidents year-wise. He finally says: "The Hindus not only reformed their systems on the basis of the Buddhist practices, they also appropriated the Buddhist shrines in due course, and replaced the Buddhist images with those of Hindu gods and goddesses".[24]

According to Neo-Buddhist scholar Ahir, the growth and decline of traditional Buddhism in India could be classified into definite periods. He says that Buddhism passed through the following periods:[25]

(1) Consolidation — 487 to 275 B.C.
(2) Systematic Propagation — 275 to 200 B.C.
(3) Popular Religion — 200 B.C. to 500 A.C.
(4) Struggle for Survival — 500 to 700 A.C.
(5) Decline — 700 to 1150 A.C.
(6) Dark Age — 1150 to 1800 A.C.

We presume the Buddha's enlightenment onwards and till his death the growth of Buddhism is taken for granted. Then one would certainly see eye to eye with Ahir on his classification, except for Dark Age which seems to continue till the end of 19th century (at least till 1891 when Ven. Anagarika Dhammapala arrived in India). We may add two more periods thereafter:

(7) Systematic revival — 1891 to 1956
(8) Sporadic revival or Mass Movement (Neo-Buddhism) — 1956 onwards

According to Ahir, In the *Consolidation Period* (487-275 B.C.) the teachings of the Buddha were codified and the Buddhist canons were formed and finalised. After the passing away of the Buddha, his teachings were assimilated, scrutinized and then canonised at the councils (*Sangiti*) at Rajgriha and Vaishali. Authenticity of the Master's teachings were declared.

In Ahir's analysis of what he terms as *Systematic Propagation,* Buddhism was made State religion by Emperor Ashoka. Buddhist missionaries were sent to various parts of India and abroad. Emperor Ashoka convened the third Buddhist Council at Pataliputra and he erected rock and pillar edicts.

The years between 200 B.C. and 500 A.C. (Ahir and other Buddhists prefer A.C. to A.D.) saw Buddhism as a 'popular religion'. Noteworthy kings had embraced Buddhism during this period. Notable among them were the Greek king Menander (also known as Milinda) and the Kushan king Kanishka. Major Buddhist works came out during this period.

The period between 500 A.D. to 700 A.D., Ahir rightly calls 'struggle for survival'. The Gupta Empire had disintegrated by then after the Hunas had come to power. Ahir says: "The successive invasions of the savage Hunas in the 5th century desocialised and destroyed almost all Buddhist places of worship in the North West India. In Kashmir, the Buddhist were mercilessly persecuted by Mihirkula, a Huna chief who came to power in 515 A.C.".[26] Nevertheless Buddhist rulers like Harsha kept Buddhism still popular.

The period of 'decline' (700-1150 A.D.) began with the demise of Harsha. The last rulers to patronise Buddhism were Patas and after their fall, Buddhism hit its lowest ebb.

Ahir continues to present that 'The Dark Age' (1150-1800 A.C.) is the period when Buddhism, already declining, suffered yet another severe onslaught by the invading Mughal army. The Mughals destroyed monasteries and killed the monks wherever they went.

Ahir brings out other good reasons for the downfall of Buddhism. The Bhikkus, he notes, had become objects of vendetta, ridicule and mockery. Even pacific monks were looted, teased and manhandled for no rhyme nor reason. On the contrary, there were internal reasons too, like lack of missionary zeal among the Buddhist monks, absence of any organisation for Lay Buddhists, lack of religious rites and rituals and inclusion of Hindu gods and goddesses by the Mahayanists are other reasons brought out by Ahir.[27] He has something more to say, namely, "Dark age was the darkest. During this period thousands of Buddhist viharas, stupas and monasteries were destroyed and plundered by the opponents of Buddhism on the one hand, and completely ignored and allowed to decay by the masses on the other hand. To which extent the Buddhist sacred shrines were neglected and even desecrated by the people of Varanasi, the Hindu holy city, can be judged from the fact that Ashoka Stupa at Saranath was dismantled in 1794 by Jagat Singh, the Dewan of Raja Chet Singh of Banaras (Varanasi) merely for the bricks required for the construction of a market in Varanasi. This market is now known as Jagat Ganj. A good number of Buddhist temples were converted into Hindu or Muslim places of worship. These included the Mahabodhi temple at Bodhgaya which was occupied by a Hindu in the 17th century. Thus, by and by, even trace of Buddhism was effaced from the land of brith".[28]

We may continue where Ahir left. The Mughal invasion and the political intrigues that followed left too little a time for the kings of various states. The rise and establishment of the British Empire in India was further a factor for relegating Buddhism in India to near oblivion. The Christian Missionary Enterprise had begun by the end of 17th century, by which time the diaspora of the Buddhist monks were complete and the stranded Laity had gone back to Hinduism. We must note that despite Mughal oppression, Hinduism was too large a religion to be wiped out. We must also note that while Buddhism lost ground, casteism once again thrived. The position of women went down again so that even evil practices like Sati and female infanticide were imposed on them ruthlessly. These factors, kept Buddhism in the oblivion till 1891, i.e., until Ven. Anagarika Dhammapala arrived in India.

There is yet another subtle reason for the fall of Buddhism which is pointed out by Jawaharlal Nehru "... It must also be remembered that Hinduism was at no time replaced by Buddhism...Brahminism and Buddhism reacted on each other, both in the realm of popular philosophy and popular belief. The Mahayana especially approached the Brahminical systems and forms. It was prepared to compromise with almost anything, so long as its ethical background remained. Brahminism made Buddha, an avatar, a God. So did (Mahayana) Buddhism. The Mahayana doctrine spread rapidly but it lost in quality and distinctiveness, what it gained in extent. The monasteries became rich and centres of vested interests and their disciples became lax. Magic and superstition crept into popular forms of worship. There was a progressive degeneration of Buddhism in India after the first millennium of its existence...Some degraded forms of Buddhism continued in East Bengal and Sind in the North West. Otherwise Buddhism gradually vanished as a widespread religion from India".[29]

As we continue to trace the fall of Buddhism in India, specially with regard to the period called by Ahir as the Dark Age, and relating this to the observations of Pandit Jawaharlal Nehru, we should note that despite the sprouting of Mahayana form of Buddhism, the Mughal attack was too much for the existence of Buddhism. Prof. Vijayakumar puts it candily: "Muslim conquest gave final death blow to Buddhism. In the eleventh century Bakhtiar Khilji of the Khilji dynasty destroyed the libraries of Nalanda and Odantapuri. This was the greatest loss Buddhism suffered. The killings that followed the Muslim conquest wiped out the Buddhist Sangha and the great teacher's (the Buddha) memory lived only as that of an Avatar— the God who came in the form of mercy".[30]

Scholar-monk, Ven. Bhikku Badanta Anand Kausalyayan in his article 'How India lost Buddhism' attributes that in addition to various reasons, factions among Buddhists which led to dubious interpretation of the genuine teachings of the Buddha, led to moral laxity among the monks and *tantriks*; also the persecutions which were meted out on the Buddhists in the 12th century led to dispersion of the monks to Tibet and other places outside India. Ven. Kausalyayan goes on to add that if the persecution on the Hindus did not extinguish Hinduism, it was because the Hindus comprised not only priests but also laymen; whereas the orange-coloured monks were easily identifiable and there was no laity to protest.[31]

Here we may emphasise lack of religious brotherhood rites and rituals as substantial reasons which would have stood out to bind Buddhists together as in the Indian context, where the Hindu environment was full of rites and rituals leading to a strong sense of solidarity amongst the Hindu neighbourhood. For this sense of solidarity exemplified by a few cases of martyrdom, Hinduism could not be obliterated by the sword and lances of the invaders, specially the Mughals.

As we close this section, we may quote Ven. Bhikku Badanta Anand Kausalyayan: "Amongst many arresting events that mark the religious histories of the world, perhaps none stands out more conspicuous and certainly none more melancholy than the disappearance of the religion of the Buddha from the land of its birth".[32] The cultural closeness of all Indians—within the orthodox systems of Indian religions (philosophical, metaphysical and spiritual) and heterodox systems (as they came to be classified later on), led to religious synchratism. Jainism had its own identity and lingered on but Buddhism could not maintain its identity as it was a case of Brahminism 2versus Buddhism, which was never a case with Jainism. Buddhism settled well outside India and Buddhists grew in number there. But in India, either the Buddhists lost their own identity and came to be embodied into Hinduism or they remained so silent that there could be only negligible number and that too nominal as the nineteenth century drew to a close.

REFERENCES

1. Pande, G.C., *Studies in the Origins of Buddhism*, (Allahabad, University of Allahabad, 1957), p. 371.
2. Oldenberg, Hermann, *Buddha, His Life, His Doctrine, His Order*, (Delhi-Varanasi Indological Book House, 1971), pp. 71-73.
3. Ambedkar, Dr. B.R., *Buddha and His Dhamma*, (Bombay, Siddharth College Publications, 1957), Introduction, p. ix.
4. Oldenberg, Hermann, *op. cit.*, p. 100.
5. Nandasara, Ven. Pt. Hegoda, *Lectures Delivered in England*, (London, Daya Henavitanse), p. 9.
6. Pande, G.C., *op. cit.*, p. 380.
7. Thomas, Edward J., *The History of Buddhist Thought*, Routledge & Kogan Paul Ltd., London, 1967, pp. 116, 138.
8. Ahir, D.C., *How and Why Buddhism Declined in India*, Mahabodhi Society of India, New Delhi, 1978, pp. 9-10.
9. Bapat, *2500 Years of Buddhism*, Publications Division Ministry of I & B, Government of India, New Delhi, p. 33.
10. Ambedkar, Dr. B.R., *The Rise and Fall of Hindu Woman*, Bheem Patrika Publications, Jalandhar, 1977.
11. Joshi, C.V., *2500 Years of Buddhism*, p. 24.

12. Edwards, Michael, In the *Blowing Out of a Flame*, George Allen & Urwin Ltd., London, 1976, pp. 45-47.
13. Saunders, L.J., *Gotama Buddha*, CLS, Madras, 1959, p. 65.
14. The Buddhist Society of India, A.P. Branch, Hyderabad, 1978 (Special Publication), Inner Page.
15. Pande, G.C., *op. cit.*, pp. 390-91.
16. *Ibid.*, p. 390.
17. Shaw, Prof. Ahmed, *Buddhism and Christian Faith*, (Lucknow Publishing House, Lucknow), 1973, p. 51.
18. Sastri, H.L.N., *The Two Aspects of Buddhism—Metaphysical and Popular*, Deep, 1968, pp. 37-38.
19. *Ibid.*, p. 37.
20. Joshi, C.V., *2500 Years of Buddhism*, p. 37.
21. Ven. Bhadant Anand Kausalyayan, *How India Lost Buddhism*? Deep, Nagpur, 1961, p. 17.
22. *Ibid.*, p. 18.
23. Ahir, D.C., *op. cit.*, p. 65.
24. Ahir, D.C., *How and Why Buddhism Declined in India*, Mahabodhi Society of India, New Delhi, 1978, p. 55.
25. Ahir, D.C., *Buddhism in Modern India*, Bhikku Niwas Prakashan, Nagpur, 1972, pp. 17-22.
26. *Ibid.*, p. 20.
27. Ahir, D.C., *op. cit.*, pp. 17-28, 63.
28. Ahir, D.C., *op. cit.*, p. 22.
29. Nehru, Jawaharlal, *The Discovery of India*, (The Signet Press, Calcutta), 1946, pp. 200-02.
30. Vijayakumar, W.R., 'A Historical Survey of Buddhism in India', *Ambedkar and the Neo-Buddhist Movement*, M.M. Thomas & T.S. Wilkinson (ed.), CISRS-CLS, 1972, p. 14.
31. Kausalyayan, Bhadant Anand, *op. cit.*, pp. 13-19.
32. *Ibid.*, p. 13.

2

THE RESURGENCE OF BUDDHISM

THE 19TH CENTURY BACKGROUND

Buddhism, which virtually vanished from the land of its birth, took deep roots in the Asian countries it had settled either in the Mahayana form or Hinayana or, for that matter, Zen Buddhism, etc. Would it ever come back as an established way of life or as a missionary religion as Emperor Ashoka had done? This might have been the fervent prayer of the faithful few who had lived and had been living here and there in India.

The question mark was big, for the caste systems had regained their fullest shape, probably stronger than before. This is quite possible, for when the Christian missionary enterprise began in India in the 17th century, the easy converts were from the low caste who wanted identity as dignified human beings and not slaves under the tyranny of caste system. We note from history that the British rulers could not or rather opted not to touch any of the social evils, lest they incur the displeasure of the people of higher castes. Caste system enforced a clear pecking system. If we see a poultry farm, we would notice the strongest hen pecking the stronger hen, the stronger hen pecking the strong hen; the strong hen pecking the weak hen and the poor and weak hen bearing the brunt of the strong, stronger and the strongest hens. The outcastes were treated at times worse than animals. Reportedly in some parts of India they were to tie a broom behind their hips to sweep their footprints and were to hang a tin round their neck lest their saliva would spill on the ground and pollute. In the caste system, the Brahmins were deemed to be of the highest order and thus exercised superiority over the next in order—the Kshatriyas. The Kshatriyas who had to be content under the Brahmins unleashed their superiority over the Vaisyas and below. The Vaisyas paid obeisance to the Brahmins and the Kshatriyas, but could assert themselves over the Sudras. The Sudras, the fourth caste in order, were subservient to the three above but yet were superior to the out-castes—the poor Panchamas or Adi Sudras or the untouchables—the real down-trodden.

The caste system even tampered with the then judiciary. As Ahir points out "even the punishments for secular offences were based on the principle of inequality, the Brahmins getting the minimum and the Sudras, the maximum punishments. Thus the entire social structure was based on the principle of inequality".[1]

The codification of Sage Manu, which was intended for administrative purposes thus took an ugly turn to establish the supremacy of one caste over the other. Referring to the caste system, Nehru writes: "The evil consequence of ceremonial purity was a growth of exclusiveness, touch-me-notism and of not eating and drinking with people of other castes. This grew to fantastic lengths unknown in any other part of the world. It led also to certain classes being considered untouchable because they had the misfortune to do some kinds of essential work which were considered unclean. The practice of normally feeding with one's own caste people spread to all castes. It became a sign of social status and the lower castes stuck to it even more rigidly than some of the higher ones...."[2] He goes on to write, "caste, which was necessary and desirable in early forms and meant to develop individuality and freedom, had become a monstrous degradation, the opposite of what it was meant to be, crushed the masses....".[3]

A corollary of this caste system in its evil form was the position of a woman in the Hinduism. While the honour bestowed on motherhood was equated with the honour due to one's motherland, but the woman even as a mother was despised. To quote Nehru again on the position of women "...Lacking most of other ways distinguishing themselves, living a confined and restricted life, they were told that their supreme virtue lay in chastity and the supreme sin in a loss of it. Such was the man-made doctrine but man did not apply to himself." Tulsidas's famous epic, *Ramcharitmanas*, written during Jehangir's time, painted a picture of woman which is grossly unfair and prejudiced".[4] In the caste system which is graded inequality, we find an element of equality with regard to the harassment of women, like female infanticide, Temple prostitutes and the horrible *Sati* —the pathetic widow-burning. Scholar and Lieut. General Sir John MacMann in his writings says, "The custom (Sati) which dates from the period of reconstructions (Re-enforcing the caste system) at least is an injunction in the *Vishnusmriti* or Tradition of Vishnu and runs thus: If a woman's husband dies let her lead a life of chastity or else mount the pyre. The presumption is that the life of chastity was so difficult that the pyre of fire was preferable.... The woman would seat herself on the pyre, with her husband's head on her lap....would then be held down on the pyre with long poles so that there would be no weakening of resolution.... Little child widows whose marriage has not been consummated must follow the same rule..."[5] Thus on the whole we find a process of human degradation, degeneration and distortions on the very essence of existence of a human being—low in the order of caste, and woman, whichever caste she may belong to. In a seminar at Hyderabad, Buddhist Subbiah read thus: "A chandala—an outcaste born to a Sudra man and a Brahmin woman had to keep a distance of sixty four cubits when he saw a Brahmin and even the Vedantist Adi-Sankara seems to have been particular about his distance when he saw at Varanasi a chandala coming his way".[6] Historian Kenneth Latourate observes, "Hinduism and caste have been so closely related, as to be almost, even though not quite, inseparable".[7] He further notes that the caste system has "condemned to ostracism and degradation those so low in its scale as to be beneath the caste structure, 'the Panchamas'. 'the Pariah' the outcastes or the untouchables".[8] We can go on quoting scores of statements by scholars and humanists on the evils of the caste system. Suffice as it would seem for our study that the caste system is vicious in its approach to the lower strata of the society and women.

Needless to mention, in this pecking order of caste system, Brahmins held their sway over all the castes: and the outcastes were the worst hit. History was to record that in the 20th century, a versatile and a volatile man would shoot forth from the very 'Panchamas'—the outcastes and in quest of human dignity would embrace Buddhism for an answer and liberate lakhs of outcastes of his sect which gave sudden boost and identity to the community and in doing so the strength of the Buddhist population in India would swell by over 1671.70 percent in a single day: But till that day—the advent of Baba Sahib Dr. B.R. Ambedkar—what was happening? The answer is rather ironical, that a

Buddhist monk had to come from Ceylon (Sri Lanka) to which Ashoka had sent Buddhist missionaries to propagate Buddhism to revive, resurge or rekindle Buddhism in India!

PRE-AMBEDKAR REVIVAL EFFORTS

It is difficult to assess the numerical strength of those professing Buddhism in its hay-days, nor it is possible to numerically visualise its strength when the decline began from 700 A.D. Nevertheless as the future archaeological discoveries were to prove, Buddhists lived throughout the Indian soil geographically before the Indian Independence —Northeast (specially Tibet); South including present Karnataka and very specially Andhra Pradesh; and of course Uttar Pradesh and Central India. The relics of the parts of the Buddha, relics of his disciples, stupas, the Lion Capital, the Dharma Chakra and edicts were excavated. The famous Ajanta caves were discovered by sheer chance by two British soldiers on patrol duty.

All these points to the glorious days of Buddhism and its related culture which gives a positive indication that Buddhism—as a religion—must have had enormous following. But consequent to the re-establishment of casteism, the persecution to Buddhism began and Buddhism was on the wane. Adding to the Mughal invasion, Buddhism as a way of life got obliterated in pre-Independence India and Buddhist viharas got dilapitated and were in ruins eventually. As Ambedkar puts it, "the present Hinduism about a thousand years ago was nothing but Buddhism but due to Moslem invasion and other causes it lost its purity and was mixed with dross".[9] Despite all this, W.W. Hunter, way back in 1893 predicted that "The revival of Buddhism is always a possibility in India. The life and teaching of Buddha are also beginning to exercise a new influence or religious thought in Europe and America... A revival of "Buddhism, I repeat, is one of the present possibilities in India".[10] This possibility became a reality a few decades later.

It began in the 19th century when a few people of the outcaste stock, specially from South India were eager to revive Buddhism; the arrival of Anagarika Dhammapala from Ceylon (Sri Lanka) was a turning point in this revival movement; the ultimate revival factor was Dr. Ambedkar himself.

Ahir states: "The history of the revival movement can be conveniently divided into three distinct phases, namely (a) Renaissance (1750-1890), (b) Systematic Revival (1891-1947) and (c) Mass Movement".[11] He goes on to narrate[12] the various archaeological discoveries made in the 18th and 19th centuries of various Buddhist inscriptions, edicts, stupas, relics and many other excavations of Buddhist interest in many parts of India, Pakistan and Bangladesh. He also points to the painstaking studies of the research in deciphering the inscriptions and the various books published by Western archaeologists like Captain Polie, Captain James Hoare, Major James Todd, Lt. T.S. Burt, James Princep, Sir Walter Elliot Forrest, Sir Alexander Canningham, Capt. Leigh, and many others including the Indian Archaeologist Dr. Bhagwan Lal Indraji. He also brings out the literary contributions of scholars like Winternitz, E. Burnouf, Fansboil, Princep, Karn, Cosma de Kores, Oldenburg, Poussin, Levi, Stcherbatsky and Mr. & Mrs. Rhys Davis. All these basically are of archaeological interest and studies on Indology. Could these be considered as part of the revival of Buddhism in India is a question to be asked.

In 1873 there was a famous debate— 'Buddhism and Christianity fact to face'— at Pandura in Ceylon, between the Buddhist monk Migethuwatte Gunananda and the Wesleyan clergyman David D' Silva which went on for two days.[13] (The proceedings of the public dabate was publicised by J.M. Pebbles in 1878.) It was the study of this debate that influenced H.S. Olcott and Mme. Blavatsky in their decision to go to Ceylon to study Buddhism. In 1880 they both became Buddhists in a public ceremony held in Galle, Ceylon.[14]

Another person to be deeply affected by the Pandura Public Debate was a young student of St. Thomas College, Colombo, whose name was David Hewavithorne, who was later to become the pioneer Buddhist missionary to India.[15] At the age of 18 Hewavithorne decided to become a Buddhist monk and to dedicate his life for the propagation of Buddhism in India".[16] "He had taken a name Anagarika Dhammapala when he became a Buddhist monk. He was born in 1864 and studied Buddhism under Bhikku Migetuwatte of 'Pandura Debate' fame".[17] His first visit to India was in 1884 along with Col. Olcott and Mme. Blavatsky at Adyar Madras.[18] In 1891 he founded the 'Budgaya Mahabodhi Society' at Colombo and when he returned to India in the same year he shifted its head quarters to Calcutta, from where he visited all over the country.[19] Inspired by Sir Edwin Arnold's articles on Budgaya he visited Saranath and Bodh Gaya in January 1891 to see for himself the condition of the Buddhist shrines. He was shocked to see the horrible condition of the most sacred shrines. The Mahabodhi Temple was being shamefully neglected and desecrated. He, therefore, resolved to restore the sacred shrines to their former glory and to make them living centres for Buddhist culture. He also resolved to regain the control of the Mahabodhi Temple from the Saivite Mahant, whose ancestors had converted it into a Shiva Temple around the close of the 17th century. With this object in view, he established the Mahabodhi Society in Ceylon on the 31st May 1891... He also decided to organise an International Buddhist Conference. This conference was held at Bodh Gaya on 31st October 1891. The representatives from Ceylon, China, Japan and Chittagong (Bangladesh) attended this conference..."[20] He also represented Buddhism at the World Parliament of Religions at Chicago in 1893. There he spoke on world's debt to Buddha and was hailed as one of the most popular speakers of that Assembly.[21] His impact in the USA is obvious in one of the letters of Swami Vivekananda who also attended the Parliament of Religions at Chicago. In a letter addressed to Mrs. Bull of the USA, Swami Vivekananda wrote: "... From what I have seen my sympathy is rather for the English Church Missionaries in India than either the Theosophists or the Buddhists. I am glad that Mr. Dharmapala has become somebody in America. Here, India is a bad place for him— I would advise him to remain in America where he may find a following. There is absolutely no hope for Buddhism in India. Again please do not be started with what the Mahabodhi paper or Missionary papers talks. These papers have no more hearing in India than what any peasant talks to his wife in private has and no more publicity..."[22] While Swami Vivekananda's letter proves Anagarika Dharmapala's popularity in the USA, history was subsequently to disprove his opinion that there is no hope for Buddhism in India. On his return to India Dharmapala launched the Bodh gaya Movement and for the first time in the history of Modern India celebrated the *Vesak* at Calcutta in 1856, with the generous help given by Mrs. Mary Foster of Hawaii, an American philanthropist. Subsequently a number of colleges and hospitals were founded in North India. Dharmapala with the help of Ashutosh Mookerjee introduced Pali studies in the University of Calcutta. This marked the great step forward in the revival of Buddhism in North India.[23] He brought from time to time many Buddhist monks from Ceylon commissioning them to various parts in the country for the propagation of Buddhism. He encouraged literary works on Buddhism. Apart from renovation of many Buddhist shrines, he built viharas also. The first vihara to be built by the Mahabodhi Society of India in the magnificent Sri Dharmarajika Chaitya Vihara in Calcutta which was opened in November 1920.[24] In 1931, the beautiful Mulagandhakuti Vihara was built at Saranath at a huge cost by the Mahabodhi Society. He decided to make Saranath a living centre of Buddhist learning and culture. For this purpose he established a library also to which, Pandit Sheo Narain, a pioneer Buddhist from Punjab, transferred all books in his personal library. Anagarika Dharmapala who had assumed the name of Sri Devamitra Dharmapala on entering the Sangha in 1931, passed away in 1933.[25] Surely, he had set in the spirit of the revival of Buddhism in India during his sojourn on earth.

In South India the revival of Buddhism which was, again, in the late nineteenth century, seems to be spontaneous awakening of a few scholars, foremost among them was Pandit Ayodhi Doss, who was an outcaste by birth (pariah—lowliest among the Tamils), a renowned scholar of Tamil literature and a society osteopath.[26] He can be compared with Mahatma Phooley for his crudes to eradicate untouchability. Vijayakumar vividly narrates the developments in South India regarding revival of Buddhism.[27] In 1894, Olcott took Ayodhi Doss to Ceylon and there Ayodhi Doss became a Buddhist and Krishnaswamiar, who accompanied them, also became a Buddhist. In 1900, Pandit Doss founded the South India Sakya Buddhist Association with its headquarters in Madras. Later it was changed to South India Buddhist Association with branches all over the State. His most important work "*Buddharathu Adivedam* (Buddha's ancient religion) is a standing testimony to his scholarship and erudition. It was at his request that the then Government of Madras separated Buddhists from others in the census of 1910. Till his death which occurred in 1914, Doss rendered yeoman service to the cause of spreading Buddhism and converted thousands of untouchables to the new faith. Notable among the associates of Doss were P. Lakshmi Narasu. Appadurai and M. Singaravelu. Narasu was well known in Japan and Czechoslovakia as the author of *Essence of Buddhism*. Ambedkar hailed it as the best book on Buddhism that has appeared so far. In addition to *Essence of Buddhism*, Narasu wrote *What is Buddhism*, *Buddhism and Hindu Religion* and *A Study of Caste*. Narasu conducted meetings to help understand the Buddhist texts. During his lifetime, he convened four Buddhist conferences and spread Buddhism among the Tamils notably among the untouchables.

We have noted the contribution for Buddhist revival in South India by modern Buddhists Pandit Ayodhi Doss, P. Laxmi Narasu, and Appadurai. We must comment on one more name, namely, that of Periyar E.V. Ramaswami Naicker, affectionately called *Periyar*. He had bred a band of young intellectuals and artists with a bent on politics. Periyar was a rationalist—his followers likened him with Ingersoll — had leaned towards Buddha as a philosopher—guide, patronised Buddhism through his political organ *Viduthalai*—which brought out the essentials of Buddhism regularly in its weekly, but plunged deeply into State politics. Periyar in late years is more remembered for his polemic anti-Brahmin activities and smashing idols and temples, projecting more on the elevation of non-Brahmins in general, but *not of* scheduled castes in particular. He was an atheist in his belief and conduct; he began more as an agnostic, who was taken to Buddha, and not Buddhism. His political party which was called Dravida Kazhagam, got split into a purely political party called Dravidar Munnetra Kazhagam (DMK) led by the late C.N. Annadurai and at present by M. Karunanidhi and further split into Anna Dravidar Munnetra Kazhagam (ADMK, now called AIADMK - 'A' and 'I' standing for All India) led by the late M.G. Ramachandran. Nevertheless, suffice it would be to say that in the fifties, the contribution of the late politician, Periyar E.V. Ramaswami Naicker was noteworthy to the cause of Buddhism in South India. The leadership of Ayodhi

Doss and subsequent outcaste leaders, led to the revival of Buddhism in South India and along with it the number of the Buddhist population soared high.

It was not all in Madras alone. Buddhism made significant progress in Kerala with the conversion of C. Krishnan, Editor of *Mitavadi*, who was elected President of the Kerala Buddhist Association established in 1925 with headquarters at Calicut. Bhikshu Dharmakhanda, a Malayali monk trained in Ceylon helped Krishnan and his colleagues in taking *Dhamma* to the masses in that State.[28]

In the Eastern, Northern, Central and Western parts of India, despite many archaeological excavations of interest to the Buddhist world, the positive revival movement took shape only after the advent of Anagarika Dharmapala with his headquarters at Calcutta. After his arrival in India for the second time, this time on permanent missionary work to propagate the Dhamma in 1891(probably in early January), he first hastened to visit Saranath and Bodh Gaya in January 1891 itself.[29] In 1892 he started the *Mahabodhi Journal* `to proclaim the doctrine glorious'.[30] He appeared to have been constantly shuttling between India and Ceylon, and everytime to add something more to the cause of Buddhism—either bringing monks for priestly work or renovation of temples, and organising conferences, etc. In 1891 Ven. Kripasaran Mahasthavir, a Bengali Buddhist monk, founded the Bengal Buddhist Association (Dharmankur Sabha).[31] About the same time Yen Mahavira, the first Indian to become a Bhikku took up his residence at Kushinagar,[32] the site of the Mahaparinirvana of the Buddha. At that time Kushinagar was in India. In fact, it was a haunted place, and people were afraid of going there. Mahavir Swami's arrival, therefore, made Kushinagar an accessible shrine. In a nutshell, the wheel of Dharma Chakra had started moving slowly — but steadily in Northern parts of India since 1891.

While the Western scholars had been regularly contributing volumes of research in Buddhism and Buddhist excavations, Indian scholars founded in Calcutta the 'Buddhist Text Society' and published many Buddhist texts in regional languages.[33] In 1900, along with Madras, another branch of the Mahabodhi Society was opened at Kushinagar and at Kushinagar the first Buddhist Vihara was built by Swami Mahavira in 1902. Thus we see that Kushinagar, once a sacred place, then a haunted place, became finally a firm Buddhist centre in this century.[34] In 1903, Kripasaran Mahasthavir founded the Dharmankur Vihara at Calcutta... In 1904, the famous Ashoka Pillar, the Lion Capital of which has been adopted as National Emblem, was discovered at Saranath.[35] The first two decades of the 20th century say excavating of great Buddhist importance. In 1920, the magnificent Sri Dharmarajika Chaitya Vihara was opened in Calcutta... The Dharmarajika Vihara, being the headquarters of Mahabodhi Society, has over a number of years become a symbol of the Buddhist revival movement in India.[36] There was yet another important convert to Buddhism. Ven. Bodhanand Mahasthavir became a Buddhist and a Buddhist monk in 1914 and was consecrated in the presence of Anagarika Dharmapala by Ven. Kripasaran Mahasthavir; the ceremony was performed in a boat on the Ganges near Calcutta.[37]

In the Western part of India, Dr. Anandrao L. Nair and Dharmananda Kosambi pioneered the revival movement and to Dr. Nair goes the credit for founding the Buddha Society at Bombay in 1922 and building the first Buddhist Vihara called Ananda Vihara in Bombay in 1931. There were two organs of the society —'Buddha Purnima' and 'Dharma Chakra'. To Dharmananda Kosambi goes the credit of being the first scholar of Pali and for building the 'Bahujana Vihara' at Parel, Bombay. Another name worthy of mention is that of Prof. N.K. Bhagat.[38] His zeal and genuine endeavour coupled with the excitement of archaeological excavations of Buddhist interest and a natural quest for spiritual satisfaction in Buddhism by native Indians of the late Pandit Ayodhi Doss in the South, Ven. Kripasarar Mahasthavir in the East, Dr. Anandrao Nair in the West and Pradhand Mahasthavir in the North, led to the Buddhist resurgence in India.

We cannot help but compare the conversion element in the then Buddhism with the same element in Christianity of the same time, only to find that in Buddhist conversion it is more a response of rationalists than the traditionalists to embrace Buddhism for soul satisfaction and not to "flee from the wrath to come" as was the thrust in Christianity. It must also be noted that the outcastes who embraced Buddhism got a separate identity for themselves free from the caste system for good. Then census had to allocate a separate column for the Buddhists. Buddhism again came into a definite being in the land of its birth. W.W. Hunter when he said in 1893 that "the revival of Buddhism, I repeat, is one of the present possibilities in India", little would he have thought that his was a prophecy:

Buddhism having come back to stay, anything connected with Buddhist holy elements (like relics) the nation noted with great interest. The national movement for freedom, having achieved independence, selected the lion capital of Emperor Ashoka as its national emblem included Dharma Chakra in the National Flag and Buddhist shrines became places of worship in the truly priestly order. In the pre-Independence period, in addition to those earlier, in 1939 a Vihara was constructed in New Delhi, Desangpani Temple in Assam in the same year; other Viharas constructed were those in Bangalore (1940), Agartala (1946) and Madras (1947 before August) and the Indian resurgence of Buddhism made an impact in Tibet and Ladakh too![39]

Buddhist literature was translated into Hindi by Mahapandita Rahula Sankrityayan, Ven. Bhadant Anand Kausalyayan and Ven. Jagdish Kashvad.

In this revival period too, we notice that there were some wanting elements. Col. Henry Olcot was not that serious about reviving Buddhism as he was a lay Buddhist and he was a theosophist too. Even convinced Buddhists like Ayodhi Doss and Lakshmi Narasu of Madras were laymen too and all they could do was to write on Buddhism primarily. Narasu's book on Buddhism is deemed to be an authority on the subject in modern times. May be, due to the vastness of the land, and paucity of monks, the missionary zeal of Anagarika Dhammapala and the few other monks who came from abroad could not make much impact in a Hindu-Muslim-Christianity dominated India. Their work in India was a sort of mild and pleasant breeze. The excavations of places of Buddhist importance and renovation certainly were a matter of joy and pride for almost all Indians, but to embrace Buddhism was a different matter altogether. In the 19th century there have been notable Indian converts to Buddhism and they became Bhikkus. But the census of 1951 recorded only 2487 registered Buddhists in Maharashtra. But just within 5 years thence, the Buddhist population in India could swell to 32,50,277. Till mass conversion in 1956, the work of the Buddhist missionaries was not consumerate with statistics in terms of conversion. Though many Mahabodhi Societies had been formed, and many Viharas had been built, however in spiritual matters quantity should not gain supremacy over quality. That quality Anagarika Dhammapala did provide in his missionary sojourn to the cause of Buddhism in India.

Another factor which might have slowed down the pace of revival of Buddhist movement in India, was perhaps that the Mahabodhi Society of Bengal had its Managing Committee comprised of non-Buddhists.

This was the state of affairs that prevailed in the history of Buddhism in India till Ambedkar came into the scene. On the whole, revival of Buddhism in India which began towards the end of 19th century presented a picture of lots of activities but near static growth till 1956 when Ambedkar and his fellow-Mahars became Buddhists in a public ceremony. Buddhism in India would have remained a speck in the ocean numerically, but for mass movements spearheaded by one of the greatest sons of India of all times—Dr. Bhimaji Rao Ramji Ambedkar.

REFERENCES

1. Ahir, D.C., *How and Why Buddhism Declined in India*, p. 9.
2. Nehru, Jawaharlal, *The Discovery of India*, Oxford University Press, 1985, p. 254.
3. *Ibid.*, p. 337.
4. *Ibid.*, p. 268.
5. Lieut. General Sir John MacMann, *Religion and Hidden Cults of India*, Neeraj Publishing House, Delhi, 1982, pp. 174-78.
6. G.V. Subbiah's paper titled *India Needs Buddhism. Why?* read in a seminar at Hyderabad on 11th May 79.
7. Latouratee, Kenneth, *Mission Tomorrow*, New York, Brothers & Harper, 1976, p. 55.
8. *Ibid.*, p. 60.
9. Vijayakumar, W.R., A Historical Survey of Buddhism in India, *Ambedkar and the Neo-Buddhist Movement*, p. 16.
10. *Ibid.*, pp. 14-15.
11. Ahir, D.C., *Buddhism in Modern India*, p. 23.
12. *Ibid.*, pp. 23-27.
13. Vijayakumar, W.R., *op. cit.*, p. 10.
14. *Ibid.*, pp. 19-20.
15. *Ibid.*, p. 24.

16. Vijaykumar, W.R., *Ibid.*, p. 24.
17. *Ibid.*, p. 24.
18. *Ibid.*, p. 20.
19. *Ibid.*, p. 24.
20. Ahir, D.C., *Buddhism in Modern India*, pp. 27-28.
21. Vijayakumar, W.R., *op. cit.*, p. 24.
22. Unpublished letters of Swami Vivekananda, XIV, Prabadden Bharata, Vol. LXXXIII November. 1978, p. 469.
23. Vijaykumar, W.R., *op. cit.*, p. 24.
24. Ahir, D.C., *Buddhism in Modern Times*, p. 30.
25. *Ibid.*, p. 33.
26. Osteopath —A Native Medical Practitioner.
27. Vijayakumar, W.R., *op. cit.*, pp. 24 ff.
28. Cf. *Ibid.*, p. 31.
29. Ahir, D.C., *Buddhism in Modern India*, p. 27.
30. Vijayakumar, W.R., *op. cit.*, p. 24.
31. Ahir, D.C., *Buddhism in Modern India*, p. 28.
32. *Ibid.*, p. 28.
33. *Ibid.*, p. 29.
34. *Ibid.*, p. 29.
35. *Ibid.*, pp. 29-30.
36. *Ibid.*, p. 30.
37. *Ibid.*, pp. 30-31.
38. *Ibid.*, p. 31.
39. *Ibid.*, p. 33.

3

DR. BABASAHEB BHIMRAO RAMJI AMBEDKAR

THE BACKGROUND AND ACCOMPLISHMENTS

'Neo-Buddhism' and Dr. Ambedkar are more or less synonymous in the sense Buddhism and Gautama the Buddha would be understood. In studying the *Dynamics of Neo-Buddhism*, we have to appreciate the state of Buddhism in its original form which was static more or less in India (even after its resurgence), until one person made it a dynamic force, making it possible to be reckoned as one of the living faiths in Maharashtra of today. That person was Dr. Ambedkar. But to highlight a few events in his life which were responsible to bring the best out of a man, we must write. In normal course of life he should have lived and died an untouchable menial. He, who would have been an ordinary sweeper-servant, went on to become a scholar-statesman. An untouchable having no identity by way of his religion—for the Panchamas are deemed outside the caste system—was destined to revive a religion and little did he know how his community was to be benefited by this revival for posterity and Indian Buddhism in the history of religions which was to take a new shape altogether.

Dr. Ambedkar was born at Mhow (in M.P. near Indore) on 14th April 1891 in a Mahar family. His surname as he entered the school in 1900 was Ambedvekar, but his kind Brahmin teacher, who was fond of him changed his name Ambedkar. Excepting the love shown by his Brahmin teacher* Bhimrao (Dr. Ambedkar's first name) experienced nothing but humiliation by his class fellows, his school peon and others. This emotional suffering led Ambedkar not to despair but to question 'Why'. This 'why' eventually—over the years—offered him the answer and made him to find a solution 'How'. When the barbers won't cut his hair, when he could not draw water from the well, and many such instances due to his low origin he did not deter from studying well.

Ramji, his father, might have been yet another menial from the Mahar community, had he not joined the Army. The British rule did not recognise the caste system of India—least in the Army. He became a Subedar Major (Junior Commissioned Officer). If the Britishers had allowed the caste system to exist it was due to their policy of diplomacy with regard to civilian Administration. Though Bimrao was his fourteenth child, yet Ramji could offered education for his youngest son. But what he imparted in his son more than academic education was some values taught to his children when he was conducting devotions at home—for Ramji was insisting on regular reading of the *Mahabharata* and the *Ramayana* everyday. As we read in the preface to

* History records that there have been Brahmins, who rose above caste (even at the cost of displeasure of their own community) to patronize non-Brahmins, at times even outcastes.

Buddha and His Dhamma, Bhimrao's father was convinced and inculcated into the minds of his children that though Karna and Dronacharya were of humble origin, by sheer dint of hard work and dedication one could like them rise to great heights. This deep rooted conviction that was put into the heart of young Ambedkar could have been the beginning of the success story of Bhimrao Ramji Ambedkar. His efforts to acquire recognition by learning and achieving looks like a repetition of the story of Karna and the latter part of his life sounds like the position that Dhronacharya held, wielding authority and evoking awe and inspiration. After he was sent for higher studies to the Columbia University (in the USA) by the Maharaja of Baroda, he is said to have been studying eighteen hours a day. It is possible that Bimrao was also inspired by the story of Ekalavya too. (Learning from a Guru in absentia, achieving the feat of accurate shooting even after loosing his right thumb by using his left thumb.) He knew that knowledge is common property of all if only sought and got. Wisdom is not the property of the rich exclusively, it is the poor's as well; for the mighty and the weak as well; for the high caste and the low caste as well. It reminds us of the Biblical dictum: "Ask and you shall receive; seek and you shall find; and knock and it shall be opened to you"[1] Ambedkar's thirst for knowledge never quenched. He was the first from his community to pass the Matriculation Examination. This seemingly not-so-great achievement led him to achieve greater than the greatest achievements in the field of academic excellence distinguishing in the disciplines of finance, law and sociology. Sreenivasa Ramanujan the mathematical genius of India—(a Brahmin) and Ambedkar (a Mahar) were contemporaries. With his academic distinction, he could command respect. Positions went to him. Psychology of religion finds eminence in the life of Dr. Ambedkar that he did not believe the hopes of his father that humble origin need not necessarily keep any person worthy of humiliation always.

The yoke is broken by grit, determination on perseverance painstaking and untiring will to win. The British rule did, indirectly, facilitate Ambedkar to rise to great heights beginning with his education.

The British Army comprised soldiers of all castes—brahmins like Mangal Pandey, the sepoy who triggered off the Indian War of Independence (Sepoy Mutiny of 1857), and Mahars like Ramji Sakpal. Ramji Sakpal, Ambedkar's father, had received Army education. Subsequently education was made available to all—though local discriminations on the basis of castes were quite prevalent. But Ambedkar could go abroad and earn doctorates after proven scholarship. He could become a barrister too. His voice, therefore, was heard with due respect later on. Rising high as Karna did, Ambedkar's attitude to life and the challenges he faced was what Arjuna said, *Na dainyam na palayanam* (neither humility nor running away). What an impact the daily vespers at Ramji Sakpal's house made in Dr. Ambedkar! Another observation that could be made here is that the devotional readings at home made Ambedkar a deeply religious man in his life. Even after he could rationalise the meaning of religion with his mature mind, his rationalism convinced him that religion is a must for one's life. He had said once "without religion society will perish".

To cite some of the humiliations he faced while at school. Once in the school, Ambedkar rushed to drink water, and the peon of the school probably a degree higher in caste than Ambedkar asked him to cup his palms together to enable the peon to pour water; in the school, he was asked to squat on the floor while children of the higher caste parents would be seated on the bench; once; when the teacher asked Ambedkar to write something on the blackboard, other students did not allow him to go near the board, as the other side of the board contained tiffins of the higher-caste children; he was not allowed to take Sanskrit as the second language; he was stoned and reprimanded for drawing water from a public well; his sister had to give him hair-cut, explaining that the barbers will not cut the hair of the low caste people; he and his brother were asked to drive a bullock-cart to reach a particular destination as the owner of the cart, who first refused to give them a ride later agreed to let them drive taking double fare but following the cart by foot. This concept of mystic pollution just by dint of one accidental birth in a low caste is the reason for the social rebellion that Ambedkar was to exhibit all through his life.

By and large, Indian approach to religion is on the basis of causal theory, God being the cause the universe. The rationalist in Ingersoll, turned him into an atheist; the rationalist in Bertrand Russell turned him an agnostic. There were and are scores of eminent thinkers who denounced religion for some reason or the other, as such. But Dr. Ambedkar wanted a religion that would stand the test of logic and give socially equal status for all. When he went abroad he saw no discrimination amongst the people over-seas on the basis of religion. When he returned to India, despite his extraordinarily high education he was still treated an outcaste by his fellow countrymen. The office mat would be rolled lest he tread, files would be flung on his table by the peon and he was not given shelter, even his business did not flourish—all because of his caste. Though he felt the pinch of all these, all he wanted to do was to secure within Hinduism equality or else adopt some other religion that would give him social security—equality being the prime factor. The strong religious fervour in him and his sublime spirituality all through his life should have been the outcome of the early intake of the same imbibed at home.

It is said that, even as a small boy, he was upset about his father's decision to remarry (after the demise of his mother) and he wanted to run away to Bombay, but had to remain stay put at home. He attempted to steal from his dear guardian aunt, whose purse—when he opened—contained just a small coin. He admonished himself for attempting to steal and that night he avowed himself that he will study hard and make her happy. Then on he is said to have put his heart and soul into his studies. When his father moved to Bombay, all had to stay in a single room. In the hustle, Ambedkar could not concentrate on his studies. Therefore, his father used to wake him up at two in the morning everyday and Ambedkar would study with utmost concentration, while the others slept. It was at this time, that he went through the insults mentioned earlier. The venue was Elphinstone High School. He was refused permission to take Sanskrit since it was not the privilege of untouchables. Therefore he had to study Persian. It is said that he would go to public garden during the day to study. With all these trying circumstances, he passed the Matriculation Examination. He being the firstever boy amongst his community to do so, the Mahar community organised a function to felicitate him, presided by the well-known scholar and social reformer of those days, namely Shri S.K. Bole. Shri Bole had authored a book on the life of the Buddha and Ambedkar was presented with that book. Who would have dreamt that 'Buddhism' would be the life et al for Ambedkar about fifty years thence!

Early marriage was inevitable those days. Shortly before his Matric Ambedkar was married to Ramabai, who turned out to be a wonderful wife. It is said of her that when Ambedkar wanted to save substantial amount for his shipfare for going to London, she agreed to run the domestics with minimum expenses and she did. It is also said of her that she did not disturb her husband when he was concentrating on his studies, not even telling him when their son Yeshwant fell ill one night and she managed all alone. She passed away in 1935. (In 1948, Dr. Ambedkar married Dr. Sharada Kabir as his second wife. She partnered him till his death in 1956 in his spiritual odyssey to adopt and propagate Buddhism.)

Back to Dr. Ambedkar's academic accomplishments, after he finished his Intermediate, his father expressed his inability to support him for further studies. On the advice of his well-wisher and another social reformer of those days, Shri Keluskar, he approached the Maharaja of Baroda for help. The generous king granted him a monthly scholarship of twenty-five rupees. Thus he could complete his B.A. in 1912 with English, Politics, Economics and Persian as his subjects. He seems to have studied Sanskrit and Pali on his own. After graduating, he was given a job in the State of Baroda. Hardly after joining that office, he had to return to Bombay to be at bedside of his dying father. After the death of his father, he came to know through his great well-wisher Shri Keluskar that the benevolent Maharaja Sayaji Rao Gaekwad of Baroda was sending a few students to New York for higher studies. After an interview with the Maharaja, he was selected and went to New York's famous Columbia University in 1913 as the Gaekwad scholar.

It was in the USA that Ambedkar first breathed the freshness equality. In June 1915, he received his M.A. degree and his thesis was 'Ancient Indian Commerce'. In May 1916, he read a paper at an Anthropology Seminar on 'Castes in India—their mechanism, genesis, and development', which was published in 1917 in the *Indian Antiquary*. In June 1916, he submitted his thesis for the Ph.D. degree on the topic 'National Dividend for India: A Historic and Analytical Study', which was published eight years later as a research article under the title, 'The Evolution of Provincial Finance in British India'. It is said that, "this book was so indispensable that during the Budget Session Indian Legislators used this as a reference book and to students it was a guide".[2]

As Ambedkar had completed his Ph.D. before the time specified, he went to the London School of Economics and to Gary's Inn, which he could not complete as he was recalled by the Dewan of Baroda. He was given a job with a promising career by the Maharaja of Baroda but could not avail it as again he became a victim to social ostracism by caste Hindus. Disgusted, he left for Bombay and became a stock market broker. Though his grasp of the market was greatly admired, his clients, when they came to know that he was an untouchable by birth, did not patronise him. Then he left that and joined as the Professor in Economics in the Sydenham College, Bombay in 1918. He had to suffer social ostracism even at the hands of high caste professors who objected to his drinking water from the pot kept for the professors.

Ambedkar kept himself cool, saved some money, with which and addition to the help of the Maharaja of Kolhapur and his friend Naval Bhathena he sailed for the London School of Economics. He could not afford to buy all the books he needed. So he decided to read in the library, morning through evening. He lived on three slices of sandwiches during daytime (for breakfast and lunch). The librarian who had been observing his non-stop studies in the library, came to know that Ambedkar did not stir out for lunch as he did not have more than one slice of sandwitch which he would take with water, insisted that Ambedkar should have lunch with him everyday. After all these hardships, he got his D.Sc. in Economics and became a Barrister-at-Laws. His thesis for D.Sc. was the 'Problem of a Rupee'. After finishing his studies in England he went to Germany for further studies in Economics. He returned to India after all his academic accomplishments—M.A., Ph.D., D.Sc., Bar-at-Laws, at the age of 32. He realised that all his qualifications are of no use as long as untouchability was the stumbling block—not only for himself—but also for the millions of untouchables seeking emancipation. He, therefore, dedicated himself to the cause of alleviation of his community and began the crusade. Buddhist scholar-monk Sangarakshita says: "from this time onwards it becomes increasingly difficult to separate the biography Bhimrao Ramji Ambedkar from the history of modern India".[3]

HIS MISSION

As much as it is difficult to separate biography of Ambedkar from the history of modern India, it is equally difficult to separate his political actions from his social achievements. Both are interwoven. He was 'a patriot of sterling worth'—as Gandhiji referred once. But his actions were so punctuated that Nehru referred some of them as 'virulence'. Ambedkar had seen the world and was educated under trying circumstances. He had seen poverty at its lowest ebb. He had suffered beyond words for having been born in a Mahar family. With all these, at the age of 32 he was one of the highest qualified men in India.

It should be noted that even at that time of caste consciousness there were high caste Brahmins like Shri S.K. Bole and Keluskar who befriended him and helped him in times of need; a progressive ruler, a kshatriya—the Maharaja Sayajirao Gaekwad was responsible for his scholastic feats. While he remained thankful to these noble persons throughout his life, what he saw in the majority of the environment around him was the injustice meted out on his fellow Mahars by the high caste Hindus. He wanted to redress their grievances, by removing the blot of untouchability For this goal he had to play the role of the leader and his people rallied behind him. When untouchables in the Southern States heard of him—specially Appadurai and Narasu from Madras, they too were with him. He got involved in politics, when there was demand for Indian Independence and this movement had gathered great momentum under the leadership of Mahatma Gandhi. But Ambedkar's leadership was limited to eradicating untouchability, gaining the privilege of securing drinking facilities from public places, gaining entry for the untouchables to temples. Therefore, politics for Ambedkar was only a means to an end. To achieve this end, he had to clash even with Mahatma Gandhi. He seems to have taken solemn vow that "he would try his utmost to free the millions of his unfortunate brethren from the yoke of social slavery and if he failed, he would put an end to his life with a bullet".[4]

ON THE THRESHOLD OF PUBLIC LIFE

Ambedkar's life is unique in the sense that his achievements in all walks of life he tried or tread, they were all connectional, beginning from the time he completed his academic education in India. His disciplined life has its roots in his childhood. But the real credit for this must go to his father, till the time his father expressed his inability to educate him beyond Intermediate.

Ambedkar deserves full credit for all that he went on to achieve subsequently—in pursuit of knowledge, in alleviation of the miseries of the untouchables, in shaping the Constitution of India and in reviving a near-dead religion in the land of its origin, we shall attempt to conclude in this section that when his desire to go abroad to pursue his higher education became a reality, there he experienced what it means to live in a casteless society. This experience is very vital, for, because of this, he could decide to launch a crusade for equality irrespective of caste barrier. The academic degrees behind his name, and the knowledge he possessed in the fields of Economics, Law and Anthropology, the knowledge he had of Hinduism and his command of the English language, kept him in good stead and his opponents had to listen to his points of view and pause, not to bye-pass him. Because of his participation in active politics—his opponents had to take cognisance of the genius in him on constitutional matters. Jawaharlal Nehru spotted this genius and despite the classes he had with Congress in general and with Mahatma Gandhi in particular, invited

Ambedkar to join his Government as Law Minister of Free India. Nehru said that Ambedkar was a jewel in his cabinet.

In the struggle for the emancipation of the Mahars and their social rights, Ambedkar came to the conclusion that Hinduism as a way of life cannot be the best way of life for the low-caste people in India and he decided to renounce it. He advised his fellow Mahars to denounce it too, and to look for a religion which would give all people equal status, despite birth in a particular community. This probably took the longest period of search; the most touchy aspect of his religiosity to finally perch; that which was to him an immortal name fetch—*his ultimate decision to embrace Buddhism*. This decision of his is the cause of revival of Buddhism in India, nostalgic and yet new. There might have been and might be genuises in the past and present, who excelled in various fields and faculties. But it is rare that excellence in one field is leading to yet another. In Dr. Ambedkar's life we can ascribe this rare sequence, if we carefully look into his life and mission. We have to browse through his biography to gather all information that led to his conversion of Buddhism, the advent of Neo-Buddhism and the present 'Dynamics of Neo-Buddhism'. In this attempt we will see coherence in Dr. Ambedkar's intelligence, intellect and education were used well in his struggle, rebellion, contribution, conviction, conversion and propagation.

Now as we analyze his life, let us see the events which are pointing to one prime mover and cherished goal—equality of all on the basis of fraternity and affirming dignity. As Dr. Ramteke points out, "His study in England and America fully revealed to him that the Hindu Social System would never free the untouchables. Only the constitutional safeguards would lead untouchables to a free life".[5] Further Ambedkar seems to have told himself that "my qualifications mean nothing. Untouchability is an obstacle even in my professional practice. I must work for the uplift of my community".[6] What are the sequences that led Ambedkar to embrace Buddhism and influenced lakhs of Mahars to accept Buddhism, and that this torch lit many lights all over India to be reckoned as 'Neo-Buddhism'—are facts demanding greater analytic study. We shall go about it eventwise for the better understanding of our study.

PIONEERS PROCEDING AMBEDKAR

Before we study in detail what Dr. Ambedkar did for the untouchables, we must note that since long there have been enlightened individuals and those belonging to the higher strata within the Hindu caste system, who were advocating upliftment of the social conditions of the untouchables—some of them even for eradication of untouchability. Kuber points out that "Mahatma Gandhi declared in 1920 'untouchability cannot be given a secondary place in the programme. Without the removal of that taint, Swaraj is a meaningless term'".[7] Kuber refers to Tilak who seems to have said that "he would not recognise God if he were to tolerate untouchability".[8] We had earlier referred to the schoolteacher of Ambedkar, whose name also was Ambedkar, befriended our Ambedkar, though the teacher was a high caste Brahmin. This teacher practically showed that an outcaste should not be treated as one. Ambedkar would not have become even a graduate, had not the Maharaja of Baroda granted him a scholarship for his graduate studies; he could not have dreamt going abroad for his M.A. and Ph.D. He would not have later on become a Barrister and a proven scholar of Economics, had not the Maharaja of Kolhapur and his friend Naval Bhattenha helped him financially.

There were scores of liberal minded high caste Hindus who sincerely tried for the upliftment of the untouchables. Some were bold and enterprising among the low castes. Mahatma Govindrao Phule opened the first school for untouchables in 1852 in Poona.[9]

Maharaja Sayaji Rao Gaekwad of Baroda's contribution to the cause of alleviating the plight of untouchables is given lesser laurels than he deserves. He established schools for the untouchables in 1883, which by 1891 became ten schools and in 1911, there were 242 untouchables serving in the State of Baroda.[10] He is same benevolent ruler who instituted scholarships for the untouchables the chief beneficiary of which was Dr. Ambedkar. The first All India Depressed Castes Conference which was held in March 1918 was presided over by this Maharaja Sayaji Gaekwad of Baroda appealing to the "conscience of the country for removing the blot of untouchability".[11]

Another great progressive ruler of those days with the same bent of mind towards the untouchables was Maharaja Shahu of Kolhapur with whose patronage Ambedkar could sail for London to complete his post-doctoral studies (D.Sc.) in Economics and to qualify as a Barrister. Dr. Ramteke says: "The Maharaja of Kolhapur, Shahu Chatrapati... established one free hostel for the untouchable class in an effort to raise other castes to a level of the Brahmins".[12] This Maharaja was the one who presided over two conferences for the Depressed Classes at Nagpur in 1918 and Kolhapur in 1920, and he saw in Ambedkar, "the potential for becoming an all India leader[13]. The Maharaja seems to have told the untouchables attending the conference: "You have found a Saviour in Ambedkar...I am confident that he will break your shackles. Not only that, a time will come so whispers my conscience Ambedkar will shine as a front rank leader of All India time and appeal"—How prophetic his observation was! In this conference Ambedkar addressed a large gathering for acquainting them with the political situation prevailing in the country.[14] Kuber says—and rightly so—that the Nagpur conference of 1918 "laid the foundation of Ambedkar's future work".[15]

These aforesaid noble souls apart, there were many more who did a lot to the cause of the untouchables in

Maharashtra. Vithal Ramji Shinde organised the 'Depressed Classes Society of India' at Bombay with the opening of a school at Parel on 18th October, 1906.[16] In Mengdur, Rao Sahib Ranga Rao started one school for the untouchables.[17] Kuber mentions the names of V.R. Shinde and Shivram Kamble for doing pioneering work in promoting the movement for the abolition of untouchability.[18]

Dr. Ramteke mentions the name of G.G. Agarkar as the most radical of the Brahmin reformers "who himself 8created no institution but represented the caste Hindu attitude which led to co-operation with untouchables, rather than service to the untouchables".[19] Ramteke further says: "The attitudes of caste Hindu reformers, both Brahmin and non-Brahmin, led to an encouragement of initiative among untouchables themselves. Schools were started in Berar and Nagpur areas in the late 19th century. Social Reform Associations were organised for the self-improvement".[20] Somawanshiya Samaj was started in Poona by S.J. Kamble, the Mohapa Low Caste Association was begin by Kisan Fago Barsod, and the Somawanshiya Hitachintak Mandal of Ahmednagar was started, whose leaders were Stripatrao Thosat and Pandoba Dangle.

For the first time in the political history of India the representatives of the untouchables put forth their case before Lord Montagu...some important institutions like the Panchama Kavli Abhinarthi—Abhimana Sangha, the Madras Presidency Untouchables Association. The Madras Adi Dravida Jana Sangham, the Bengal Untouchable Classes Organisation and the Depressed Classes Mission of India appeared before Lord Montagu and appealed to the British Government to protect the untouchables from the age-long slavery of the Caste-Hindus. The Congressmen soon became conscious of their existence....Under the Presidentship of Dr. (Mrs.) Annie Besant, the Congress passed the resolution: "the Congress urges upon the people of India the necessity, justice and righteousness of removing all disabilities imposed by custom upon the Depressed Classes".[21] This event took place soon after Ambedkar's return to India in 1917.

In South too, there was an awakening amongst the outcaste community—specially Pariahs (the counterpart community of Mahars) in the late 19th century. Pandit C. Ayodhi Doss, whom we had mentioned earlier as one who helped revive Buddhism in South—was an "accredited crusader against untouchability".[22] Col. Olcott, the American who came to India as seeker of truth with Madam Blavatsky started the Theosophical Society and eventually became Buddhists. When Ayodhi Doss met Col. Olcott requesting him to help revive Buddhism in South India, Col. Olcott identified himself with the lot of the Parish community, and started schools for the untouchables at Madras and colleges in 1894, 1898 and 1899 respectively. There were 384 boys and 150 girls. This movement demanding 'equality' in the then Madras Presidency, spread over to all untouchables speaking Tamil, Telugu, Malayalam and Kannada.

As the 20th century dawned, the social environment of the country was awakening to the cries of the untouchables and their voices were being heard. Aided by liberal minded caste Hindus, and patronised by Hindu rulers, the untouchables in different parts of India were demanding their rights to be treated as human beings. There were different leaders at different places amongst each untouchable communities, in different States.

At national level there could be only one forum—the Congress for the Congress leaders, by and large, had in their priorities, like equality for the untouchables, but the top priority was Swaraj or home rule, and the plight of the untouchables, though had sympathetic hearing, remained *status quo* and the outcome had to be only next to nothing. The sporadic voices crying 'equality', 'abolition of untouchability' and 'justice' in the nineteenth century would have been a voice in the wilderness, but for what the twentieth century had to offer to the untouchables—through a man among those very untouchables—Dr. B.R. Ambedkar. The struggles of the pioneers preceding him, were not a waste, but a culmination and fruition was through the untiring and brilliant leadership of Ambedkar, whose approach to the problem of untouchability was action and agitation oriented. In him the untouchables—Mahars to begin with, but subsequently all untouchables all over India found a unique leader, not less by any standards to any high caste Hindu. Ambedkar too took up the leadership unhesitatingly.

AMBEDKAR'S CONVICTIONS

Ambedkar's struggles were to achieve social justice for the Mahars. Later, Mahars became part of the many untouchables the total community of which was for Ambedkar, one unit. Their liberation from the evils of caste-system was the main, if not the only objective of Ambedkar. Ambedkar's ideal society was based on liberty, equality and fraternity. To achieve these sociological values as reality for the untouchables, active involvement in politics was a means to an end for Ambedkar. Between 1917 and 21920, when he was in India (after his return from abroad), Ambedkar realised that educated or not, civilised or not, efficient or not, all these meant nothing for an untouchable against the deep rooted caste-system in India. It was during this period that he tried to begin his independent career as a stock-broker or later a faculty member of Sydenham College. But his lowly birth could not let him establish himself. Undaunted, he found time to participate in various conferences of the Depressed Classes in Poona, Nagpur, Bombay and during these years he formulated his future dictum— 'organise, educate, agitate'. He had made up his mind to go back to England to complete his academic pursuits and therefore lived a very frugal life and his wife is said to have given her utmost co-operation to achieve this goal.

After the Sydenham College water-pot incident, Ambedkar hasted his plans to leave for England. After his return from London he launched into public life *in toto*—having only one thing in mind: 'Emancipation of the untouchables of India'. Kuber sums up the mind of Ambedkar before he launched himself into the deep sea of crusade to the cause of untouchables: "... Ambedkar realised that the impact of the West influenced Indian social and political life. He visualised that this western system alone would break the shackles of untouchables in India. He preached by his own example that 'worth' and not 'birth' shapes the life of an individual in any country*. Before he entered Indian politics he was fully equipped with the western thoughts of democracy, equality, liberty and fraternity. His study in England and America fully revealed to him that the Hindu social system would never free the untouchables from social and political oppression. It became clear to him that not the laws of many but the constitutional safeguards would ultimately lead untouchables to a free life...Ambedkar always made efforts to maintain a balance between thought and action. His principles of dynamism recognised that there is nothing fixed, nothing eternal, nothing *sanatan*: but everything is changing, that change is the law of life for individuals as well as for society..."[23] Ambedkar's reference to change as the law of life is an excerpt from his pamphlet 'Annihilation of caste'. He reflects the philosophy of Hereclates that change is the ultimate reality of life.

As we all know, there were many enlightened untouchables in the past like Kabir and Ravidas, but their lives were pointing to devotion cult. Though spiritually inspiring, they were consigned to their fate of lowly birth and their spirituality was other worldly. Namadev and Chokamela (13th and 14th century respectively) were also

* A realisation of the teaching of the Buddha.

saint-poets venerated even today. It was for Ambedkar, a scholar-politician, to fight it out in an effort to annihilate caste system. When he realised this is not possible within the Hindu fold, he switched over to the concept of equality and total human rights outside the Hindu fold. He was successful at it. What he could do for those untouchables who remained within the Hindu fold too were manifold—privileges, reservations, and the like.

Ambedkar realised that if the untouchables are to emancipate themselves, education is a must. He said: "Education is something which ought to be brought within the reach of everyone".[24]

These were the basic thoughts of Ambedkar as he took over leadership of the Mahars which was to last for another four decades.

AGITATIONS AND SOCIAL STRUGGLES

Pre-Ambedkar reformers had been appealing to people for justice and the response they could get was mere sympathy. But Ambedkar resorted to agitations and social struggles as direct actions against caste oppressions and disabilities.

Though Ambedkar's leadership of the untouchables at large began only from 1923, i.e., after his second visit abroad, yet he made his work as leader and showed his concern for the Mahars way back in 1917, i.e., after his return first visit abroad. In 1920 Ambedkar started a weekly *Mooknayak* (Leader of the Dumb) to voice the woes of the Depressed classes of India. In the editorial of the first number, he said that devoid of power and knowledge, the non-brahmins and the Depressed classes cannot make any progress.

When Ambedkar left for London in 1920, even there the cause of the untouchables was very dear to his heart. There he met Vallabhbhai Patel and Lord Montagu, (British Secretary of State for India) in 1921 and appraised them of the plight and grievances of the untouchables in India.[25] It must be mentioned that a delegation of the representatives of the Depressed Classes Association had met Montagu in 1917 with an appeal to protect the interests of the untouchables and he was sympathetic. After his return in 1923, the next three decades saw voluminous output of Ambedkar for the uplift of the untouchables and while doing so he dominated the political scene of India causing anxious moments on and off to the leaders of the Indian National Movement.

It is said that Ambedkar was behind the Civil Rights bill of 1923 moved by S.K. Bole in Bombay Legislative Council. The bill was to allow all the untouchables to use all public water places. The Bombay Government directed in September 1923 that this resolution be implemented. When some of the municipalities and Local Boards did not implement this resolution. Mr. Bole moved another resolution in August 1926 not to accord sanction of grants to such municipalities. The Municipality at Mahad threw open the water tank to all communities. The caste Hindus were all out not to allow the untouchables to avail water from Mahad tank. This was to lead to an open confrontation with the Caste Hindus. (Here we must note that Ambedkar had established the 'Bashishkrit Hitkarani Sabha' on 20th July 1924 through which he wanted to "light the fire of self-help and self-respect among the untouchables and wished to bring all untouchables under one banner".[26]) He convened a conference of the Depressed Classes at Mahad on 19th and 20th March 1927 and addressed the 10,000 delegates who attended to abandon their 'Watans'[27] (menial work in Municipality on pay for an individual, but in whose absence that work must be attended to by any other member of the family.) "He concluded that the watans were the greatest hinderance in the advancement of the Mahar community".[28] He then led all the delegates to the Chowdar water tank at Mahad to drink water so as to enforce implementation of the Bole Resolution of 1923 and to assert their right to drink water from the municipal tank. Ambedkar... "asserted the right of the suffering humanity by drinking water from the forbidden tank. Most of the Volunteers following him followed suit and vindicated their right. ...The fanatic Hindus failed to check the march of the untouchables to the tank...The unarmed men and women were mercilessly beaten up by the caste Hindus. Ambedkar advised his followers to be calm and not to retaliate—Later Mahad Municipality also revoked its resolution. This infuriated the untouchables. Accordingly a *Satyagraha* was planned for December 1927. Thousands of Satyagrahis reached Mahad on the 25th December 1927. One of the resolution related to *Manusmriti* was passed and...a copy of it was also ceremoniously burnt. The Satyagraha was planned on the 26th December. As, some Hindus had filed a suit claiming the tank as a private property, ultimately therefore, the move to launch the Satyagraha was abandoned. The chowdar tank case was later fought out in courts and won by Ambedkar."[29]

In 1927, as early as 3rd April, Ambedkar had started *Bahishkrit Bharat*, a fortnightly paper in Marathi. In that he once wrote in the editorial that "had Tilak been born among the untouchables, he would not have raised during the national movement the slogan: 'Swaraj is my birthright', but a slogan like: 'Annihilation of untouchability is my birth-right' ... Lost rights are never regained by begging, but by relentless struggle. Goats are used for sacrificial offerings and not lions".[30] 1927 and 1928 were very busy years for Ambedkar organising, presiding and addressing. He was also regular in attending Bombay Legislative Council to which he was elected in 1924. When the Simon Commission called him over to explain his standpoint in 1928, he demanded joint electorate with reserved seats in legislatures and told Sir John Simon: "We must be treated as a distinct minority, separate from the Hindu community—

the Depressed Classes minority needs far greater political protection like any other community in British India for the simple reason that it is educationally very backward, that it is economically very poor, socially enslaved and suffered from certain grave political disabilities from which no other community suffers".[31] In September 1928, Ambedkar formed the 'Samata Sanik Dal' (Social Equality Army) whose aim was to "dislodge all those values which conserved and fostered anti-human elements in the traditional and cultural heritage".[32] Earlier the same year, he had established a Depressed Classes Education Society for the educational uplift of his people. Again in 1929 Ambedkar organised successfully a strike by the textile workers, as a bill which was about to be passed deprived the poor mill labourers the right to strike work in protest.

1929 was again a year marked with activities which had far-reaching consequences. He organised and addressed many meetings and confidence inspiring and instilling confidence in the listeners, advising them to continue to struggle till they obtain their cherished goals. The most important movement was the Satyagraha launched to gain entry into the Parvati temple at Poona, which was hitherto denied for the untouchables. Some advised "wait for sometime and await the change of heart on the part of touchable Hindus" and to them Ambedkar's reply was: "Is there any sense in asking the Depressed Classes to wait any longer in establishing an ordinary human right to enter a place of worship?"[33] This Satyagraha was not successful.

Another important meeting in 1929 for the Depressed Classes movement was the meeting held at Jalgaon on 29th May 1929, where a resolution was passed *Stressing the Need for Embracing any Other Religion*. Ambedkar was touching delicate issues like religious conversion for the upliftment of untouchables during the national movement. So he advised such of them as could endure no longer the pangs of poverty, misery and disabilities, to embrace any other religion for the betterment of their lot and honour, if the disabilities were not removed by caste Hindus before a prescribed date. The path to religious and social emancipation was far steeper and less attractive. It had not yet been trodden with determined purpose by the great majority of the Hindus. From now on we see in Dr. Ambedkar a two-fold purpose of leadership, on the one hand for freedom in the socio-economic field and for freedom in the right to religious practices on the other, though in the change of religion he did not bestow much attention. The first effort was to launch a Satyagraha in October 1929 to worship deity in Parvati's temple at Poona, which we had referred to earlier. A more determined and vehement agitation was to secure entry into the Kalaram Temple at Nasik on 2nd March 1930. From 3rd March that year 8000 satyagrahis sang Bhajans and peacefully sought entry into the temple, the doors of which were closed. After a month, the administrators of the temple came forward for negotiations with the untouchable satyagrahis and offered to let the untouchables to pull one side of the chariot on Ramnavami festival. Thereupon, the satyagrahis called off the satyagraha. But on the day of reckoning, the untouchables were left deprived of the opportunity to participate in the festival by not being allowed to pull the chariot. The temple remained closed for the whole year and the agitation continued till October 1935. The year 1935 could be regarded as a decisive year in the history of religions in India, for in that year Ambedkar declared that though he was born a Hindu, he will not die a Hindu. From then on his search for an alternate religion began earnestly. Before we focus our attention on this important declaration of Yeola in 1935, it is worthwhile noting a few important events which made Ambedkar a national leader of repute and for some, controvertial. But his stature as a national leader was well established even before 1935. This period of about five years witnessed open ideological clashes between Mahatma Gandhi and Ambedkar.

Ambedkar attended the All-Parties Conference in 1928 and in 1930. His patriotism is evident from the speech he made in the 1930 at All-Parties Conference in that he "stressed the need of Hindu-Muslim unity and cohesion against the British Imperialism for uprooting it".[34]

FIRST ROUND TABLE CONFERENCE

The British Government held a Round Table Conference in London in November 1930 to frame the Constitution of India. On 8th and 9th August the same year the All-India Depressed Classes Congress was held at Nagpur. At this conference Ambedkar made good his speech on India's Self-Government as under: "A common Government is often the best instrument one can advise to mould a diverse people into nation and demand adequate safeguards of the degraded untouchables in the Constitution".[35] At this conference, it was agreed that Ambedkar ought to represent them at the Round Table Conference. Ambedkar and Rao Bahadur Srinivasan were nominated by the Government to participate in the Round Table Conference to be held in London.

For the first time the untouchables were regarded, not merely as a separate element from the Hindus, but also of such importance as to have the right to be consulted in framing of a Constitution for India. The Conference which began on 12th November 1930 comprised eighty-nine members and lasted till it was adjourned on 19th Jan. 1931. In the plenary session of the conference on the 20th November 1930 Ambedkar flayed the British rule for its apathy towards the Depressed Classes. He asked: "has the British Government done anything to remove untouchability?" and remarked: "the wrongs against the untouchables have not been righted although 150 years of British rule have passed".[36] He went on: "We must have a government in which the men in power will give their undivided allegiance to the best interest of our country. We must have a government in which men in power, knowing where obedience will end and resistance will begin will not be afraid to amend the social and economic code of life which the dictates of justice and expediency so urgently call for. This role the British Government will never be able to play. It is only a Government which is of the people, for the people and by the people that will make this possible".[37] It is said that British delegates were stunned by the strong indictment by Ambedkar. They wondered whether he was an Indian revolutionary.

The conference was divided into sub-committees and Ambedkar served on three sub-committees— (i) The Minorities sub-committee, (ii) The Provincial Constitution sub-committee, and (iii) The Services sub-committee. In all these committees, Ambedkar's contributions were excellent. For the minorities sub-committee, he drafted an 8-point scheme for protecting the safeguards of the Depressed Classes; for the Constitution sub-committee, he suggested franchise and representatives of different classes; for the Service (Defence) sub-committee, he suggested that recruitment to the services should be for all Indians.[38] After his creative participation in the First Round Table Conference, Ambedkar returned to India on 27th February 1931.

On his return to India, Ambedkar was as busy as ever, but did not have sufficient time to achieve much as the Second Round Table Conference was not very far. In April 1931, it was decided by the Depressed Classes headed by Bhanrao Gaikwad to revive the agitation for temple entry. Meetings were mobilised and Ambedkar made a stirring speech. Ambedkar convened a conference in Bombay on 14th April 1931 for considering the report about the First Round Table Conference.

MEETING WITH GANDHI

On 14th August 1931, Ambedkar met Mahatma Gandhi at the latter's behest. The meeting ended in clash of the titans, where the Mahatma and Ambedkar held opposite views with regard to separate electorates for the untouchables. This remained a bitter pill towards and for each other. This also affected the deliberations of the Second Round Table Conference held at London in September 1931. During the meeting with Mahatma Gandhi, Ambedkar asked the Mahatma to his face: "How can I call this land my own and this religion my own, wherein we are treated worse than cats and dogs, wherein we cannot get water to drink? ...As per my conscience, I have been striving to win human rights for my people without meaning or doing any harm to this country". ...Gandhi reacted "I am against the political separation of the untouchables from the Hindus. That would be absolutely suicidal".[39]

SECOND ROUND TABLE CONFERENCE

At the Second Round Table Conference in November 1931 Gandhiji claimed himself as the sole representative of India, which was not accepted. The statement of the Mahatma that "so far as the untouchables are concerned... I would strongly resist any further representation," led to Ambedkar's reply: "this is nothing but a declaration of war with Mr. Gandhi and the Congress against the untouchables. ...Whether I am a nominee or not, I fully represent the claims of my community..."[40] Response to Gandhiji's claim to represent the Depressed Classes was decried in India, and many public meetings were held in support of Ambedkar's claim. By the effort of Appadurai, founder of South India Buddhism Association, messages were sent to Prime Minister Ramsay MacDonald, the Chairman of the Round Table Conference, that "Ambedkar and not Gandhi, was their representative".[41] The Round Table Conference was adjourned on 1st December 1931 and Ambedkar returned on 29th January 1932.

SEPARATE ELECTORATE

From now on, Ambedkar had set separate electorates for the untouchables as his objective. He went again to England on 7th June and returned on 17th August 1932, after appraising the leading British politicians and ministers on the untouchables issue. The communal award was announced by the British Premier and the Depressed Classes were given separate electorates. Against this award which favoured the untouchables, Gandhiji announced that he would fast upto death from 20th September 1932 and began his fast at Yervada Jail. Ambedkar was called names, but he stood firm that he will not betray the interests of his people. When Gandhiji's condition grew worse, for the sake of humanity he agreed to the conditions of Gandhiji and Gandhiji in turn agreed to increase the seats for Depressed Classes and broke his fast. This 'Poona Pact' as it was called, subsequently did not prove a successful solution except that it saved Mahatma Gandhi's life. After this pact Gandhiji was more inclined to serve the cause of the Depressed Classes whom he called 'Harijans'. While comparing the efforts of Gandhiji and Ambedkar, Ahir says: "In his efforts to liberate the suppressed and oppressed masses Ambedkar surpassed Gandhi. He was like a mother to the untouchables where Gandhiji was like a nurse... But for him, the history of the untouchables would have been quite different".[42]

THIRD ROUND TABLE CONFERENCE

Then came the Third Round Table Conference which was held again at London from 19th November to 24th December 1932. After participating in it Ambedkar returned in January 1933. The 'Swaraj' did not come through. Subsequently, there was a dual between Gandhiji and Ambedkar on the issue of Temple Entry and the doctrine of *chaturvarna* in which they were holding diametrically opposite views. In April 1933, Ambedkar left again for England to work in the Joint Committee for Indian Constitution and returned in January 1934. But from 1st June 1935, he became the Principal of Government Law College, Bombay. Here we should note that from 1929 till 1935, the political environment was more of bitterness and very hard-going for Ambedkar, who was called during those days a British stooge and a traitor, as he opposed Gandhi.

Having been a genuine victim of social ostracism from the time of his known childhood, Ambedkar did not deter from his decision to struggle untiringly for the social uplift of his people. In doing so, he became the acknowledged leader of the Depressed Classes on Indian level and national leader too. The adverse reaction of the caste Hindus, specially at the Mahar water tank, and the Temple entry and Gandhiji's attitude towards separate electorates for the Depressed Class should have put any leader's spirit down. But the indomitable spirit in Dr. Ambedkar did not allow him to be cowed down. He remained true to his convictions and was defiant on the issue of basic human rights being denied on caste basis.

YEOLA DECLARATION

Ambedkar was an affable person and as the late Shri C. Rajagopalachary puts it, "Ambedkar was a thoroughly upright person and a man with a keen jurist sense, a proud and irreconcilable heart, great learning, and when approached in right spirit full of friendliness".[43] For such a person who was a man of conviction, when not treated well by his fellow Indians of upper castes, denied by his people what he was fighting for, dubbed a traitor and a British Stooge by his political and ideological opponents, it is but natural to get frustrated.

The past twelve years preceding 1935, whatever he achieved never came the easy way. But whatever Ambedkar endeavoured to bring in for the alleviation and amelioration of the Depressed Classes—specially the Mahars, his own community, was largely denied by the Caste Hindus of those days who were soaked and steeped in superstition, auspicion and in the devout belief in 'karma'. When the untouchables tried 'en masse' to drink water from public places the upper castes were convinced that the water *will* get polluted and their reaction to rebellion was to 'quell rebellion by force'.

Dr. Ambedkar, born amongst the lowliest of the low, but having been exposed to highest possible education abroad, was again a victim of ostracism and intimidation. Would he not react? Not only that he also was determined to uplift his fellow Mahars along with himself, his analytical mind convinced him that the woes and miseries of the Depressed Classes were due to the basic structure of the Hindu Society—the *Varnashrama Dharma*. Hence he exhorted to his people that Hinduism is not a 'Religion but a visitation' and added pungent adjectives like 'Diabolical' etc. Hindu structure then (and in unknown villages even now) was such that untouchability was—as Gandhiji analysed a 'bi-product of the High and Low'. But what mattered to Ambedkar was in society the Depressed Classes were treated 'worse than cats and dogs', deprived of basic needs like even drinking water, leave alone to imagine higher things in life and for whom efficiency, education even if attained did not matter to escape social ostracism.

Ambedkar when his efforts to bring about a change in hearts of Higher Caste Hindus and bestow the legitimate human rights for the members of his caste proved futile, he thought he would quit the religion itself. Dr. Presler observes, "Ambedkar was now painfully conscious that his efforts to obtain liberty, equality and fraternity for the Depressed Classes while within Hinduism, failed to meet his expectations, there was one last recourse that might be tried: to change his and their religion".[44]

This grave decision was the outcome of the sufferings, which he and his fellow-Mahars had been going through.

What he was craving for—both for himself and his community—self-respect and dignity was summarily denied to him in the Hindu society. Equality was not to be found in Hinduism, which was based on graded inequality. As such humiliation and despair would be the natural corollary which Ambedkar had experienced to the fullest measure. He probably might have hoped that there could be some broad-minded person like his former royal patrons—the Maharaja of Baroda and the Maharaja of Kolhapur—who would belong to the higher castes and share the responsibility of upliftment of the Depressed Classes. Though Gandhiji declared that the Congress would share that 'onus' with Dr. Ambedkar, it was only Gandhiji who uttered it and attempted it, but at the same time Gandhiji's primary goal was India's independence and the cause of removing untouchability was immediate next. This was proved shortly before when the third session of the Constituent Assembly met. Later, a bill was moved by Sardar Patel in the House which declared on April 23, 1947, that 'untouchability in any form is abolished and the imposition of any disability on that account shall be an offence".[45] For Ambedkar amelioration and upliftment of the Depressed Class was his most cherished goal primarily. Hence Ambedkar did not have full faith in Gandhiji's efforts to eliminate untouchability. When Ambedkar could not trust the genuineness of Gandhiji himself, whom else would he? Whose bonafides could he believe?

Ambedkar represents the class of people defined by an old adage— "a man convinced of his will, is of the same opinion still". Yet he idolised frank persons like Martin Luther and he quoted his example to say that he would like a man who would face the Pope and tell on his face that he is not infallible.

We can say that owing to the bitter experiences he had faced since his childhood, youth and adulthood, Ambedkar came to the firm conclusion that all that he and his fellow Mahars had been suffering all through was due to Hindu

Caste System, though he tried to assert the rights of Mahars by peaceful means. He never advocated violence. But when this did not work, he decided to avail the human rights by changing religion, knowing pretty well the stigma of being a Mahar is going to linger for a long time.

The leaders of the Depressed Classes held a Conference at Yeola (Nasik) on 13th October 1935 to review the political and social situation in the light of their fifteen-year old struggle and the ensuing Constitutional reforms. Then Ambedkar declared: "Unfortunately, I was born a Hindu untouchable. It was beyond my power to prevent that, but it is within my power to refuse to live under ignoble and humiliating conditions. I solemnly assure you that I will not die a Hindu"*.[46] Vijayakumar says: "The conference which was attended by about ten thousand people passed a resolution which read: the Depressed Classes should leave Hindu fold and join some other religion that gives social and religious equity to them...Choose any religion that gives equality of status and of treatment..." However, what religion should replace Hinduism the conference did not attempt to decide".[47] Further a resolution was passed that "now the Depressed Classes must not spend money and manpower fruitlessly and must stop the fight on Satyagraha front. They must now consider their society separate from the Hindu society and organise the former to obtain for it an independent and respectable place in the country. Henceforth, all Depressed Classes must not take part in any Hindu religious festivals, Ratha, worships and other similar occasions".[48]

These quotes mentioned above were the sum and substance of the conference at Yeola. This conference was followed by another at Poona next year, in which alternate religion was considered. Eventually it came to light, "that the immediate problem facing Scheduled Caste movement was not that of conversion but of consolidation"[49]. In this

* This declaration of Dr. Ambedkar is generally known as the Yeola Declaration.

conference it was mentioned: the Depressed Classes needed no saint, or the Vedas, or the Geeta or any Sankaracharya or any Apostle, but Ambedkar himself".[50] The inevitability of Ambedkar for the Depressed Classes could not be emphasised better and the choice of alternate religion was left to Ambedkar himself. But Ambedkar was quick to warn his people against the view that conversion will bring them equality—social or religious. He said "Go anywhere we will, we would have to fight for our welfare; so anywhere, fight is inevitably in store for us".[51]

Thus, we note that a positive decision has been taken by the Depressed Classes to go in for a new religion, renouncing their ancestral Hindu religion. Ambedkar had played up time of the 1929 resolution. But this time, he was earnest to go in for a change. His followers were willing to follow him to the core. Till the Yeola Declaration (to adapt Shakespeare's famous soliloquy in *Hamlet*), 'to be or not to be a Hindu', was the question for Ambedkar.

Now onwards, Ambedkar's subsequent contribution was more on the political side and ultimately to the cause of Buddhism in India. His forming the Independent Labour Party and winning the elections and onward till he became a Cabinet Minister of the Nehru's Government is all part of the political history of India. What is most important in the political career of Ambedkar is his selection into the Drafting Committee of the Constitution of India and his subsequent appointment as its Chairman. As he brought out the Constitution of India, he made full social security for the Depressed Classes. The following articles of the Constitution of India need special mention. Ambedkar might have had in mind the miseries he had experienced as an 'outcaste' when he drafted the articles on untouchability as under:

Articles. 15: (1), (2) (a), (2) (b);

16: (1), (2), (3), (4), (5);

17:

Ambedkar resigned from the Nehru's Cabinet as he could not get the Hindu Code Bill passed which was intended to protect the interests of Hindu women. Then he was, further, defeated in the next General Elections and passed into political oblivion. His political achievements are not easy for any one to perform in the circumstances Ambedkar was placed. It is very difficult to emulate his example too. He had withstood and weathered all kinds of storms, but he stood like the rock of Gibralter.

When he announced his decision to change his religion, he was on the one side heckled, on the other side leaders of other religion put pressure on him to come into their fold. It was only towards the end of his political 2career, he made up his mind to embrace Buddhism. The philosophy of John Dewey —utility or Pragmatism—which influenced him a lot, influenced him in his spiritual quest too. His search for another religion transformed into a spiritual odyssey.

THE SEARCH FOR AN ALTERNATIVE

Ambedkar's search for an alternate religion began as reaction or retalisation to the attitude of the caste Hindus, denying the untouchables the basic human needs—both social and spiritual. While applying the methods of appeals, requests, admonitions he never opted for violence. But what might have worked up in the mind of the agitating Dr. Ambedkar was the speech of Gandhiji at the Second Round Table Conference at London. "I do not mind untouchables, if they so desire, being converted to Islam or Christianity. I should tolerate that but I cannot possibly tolerate what is in store for the Hindus if these two divisions (caste and outcaste) set forth in the villages and therefore, I want to say with all the emphasis that I command that if I was the only person to resist this thing, I would resist it with my life".[52]

Did Dr. Ambedkar think that if Gandhi himself would prefer the untouchables to leave Hinduism so as to join another religious fold than the Caste Hindus by giving in to the demands of the untouchables, the untouchables may better change over to another religion? However, Dr. Ambedkar must have firmly decided to leave Hinduism only after the fiasco of the pact he had made with Gandhiji at the Yervada Jai in 1932. This frustration he voiced at Yeola in 1935 (Supra) that he will not die a Hindu, though he was helplessly born as one.

What are the possible alternates to Hinduism? The thought of conversion was at that time not spiritually based, but totally materialistic. It is possible that Dr. Ambedkar might not have given credence to the need of spiritual conviction before conversion, because he might have witnessed the Christian Mass Movements of those days whence the Christian Missionaries applied the policy of 'convert first; convince later'. (Genuine conversions to Christianity were very few, Brahmins like Pandita Ramabai, Fr. Nehemiah Goreh, Narayan Vaman Tilak, etc., but most of the converts were from the Depressed Class seeking emancipation socially and materially.) While thinking of an alternate religion Ambedkar thought of not only social and material needs of his people, but also he put his national interest too, for, as Gandhiji had complemented him, he was certainly a 'patriot of sterling worth'. At that stage Ambedkar did not think of the spiritual depth of any other religion which he looked for much later.

After 1935 Conference at Yeola, the response from the leaders and other religious leaders, as could be anticipated was an *apology* (defence) for Hinduism. Dr. Kurta Koti suggested that the Depressed Classes may be a Hindu new sect like Arya Samaj or Brahma Samaj with Ambedkar as its founder, so that the conversion of the untouchables could be avoided and they could get equal rights in Hindu Society.[53] Then prominent Hindu leaders like Veer Savarkar and Jayakar met him on 10th November 1935 and requested him not to implement the resolution. Gandhiji's reaction was this:

"The speech attributed to Dr. Ambedkar is unbelievable... If the conference has adopted a resolution of complete severance from Hinduism and acceptance of any faith that should generate equality. I regard both as unfortunate events. Untouchability is on its last legs. But religion is not like a cloak which can be changed at will. It is a more integral part of one's self than one's body...I would urge (Dr. Ambedkar) to assuage his wrath and to reconsider the position and examine his ancestral religion on its own merits and not through the weakness of its unfaithful followers".[54] ...When shown the Mahatma's comments he replied, "...I agree with Mr. Gandhi that religion is necessary, but I do not agree that a man must keep his ancestral religion, if he finds that religion repugnant to his notions of the sort of religion he needs, as the standard for the regulation of his own conduct and as the source of inspiration for his advancement and well being".[55]

Even the Depressed Classes communities on the whole were divided with regard to Ambedkar's Yeola Declaration and the resolution passed in the conference. One of his earliest associates of Ambedkar Kisan Fagoji Bansod, to whom the credit goes to introduce Ambedkar to Nagpur in 1926, criticised Ambedkar for his intention to convert though Bansod was also a Mahar.[56] Dr. Ramteke says: "The Depressed Classes League which was established in 1934 under the leadership of Jagjivan Ram (a Harijan) launched a campaign against Ambedkar's declaration. On November 15, 1935 Dewan Chaman Lal, the President of Punjab Depressed Classes League, termed Ambedkar's statement as a 'dangerous move'...On December 22, 1935, Mr. B.N. Mandal, too refused to side with Ambedkar at the conference of the Assam Depressed Classes League...Ambedkar was never afraid of such opposition and continued his activities...Later on, Ambedkar declared that the issue of conversion would be decided at a Mahar Conference to be held in the near future".[57]

Many more persons tried their best to coax Dr. Ambedkar to retract his decision to leave Hinduism. Ambedkar, we can say at this juncture was never adamant not to detract from his Yeola Declaration, than to say he was firm. He also must have realised that changing one's religion was not, as Mahatma Gandhi said, like changing one's cloak and he took his own time, thinking of the consequences of leaving Hinduism—may be in the light of opposition not only from the fellow Depressed Class folks, but also from some of his own fellow Mahars. He was at this stage more concerned about the upliftment of his own community and the Depressed Classes, which he came to conclude positively that it is not possible being within the Hindu fold with its caste system and which he castigated as a 'Diabolic' religion.

Ambedkar's delay in choosing the alternate religion was termed by many in different ways. For Dr. Presler the time delay was 'vacillation between Hinduism and Buddhism'[58] Sangharakshita also uses the same word 'vacillation'.[59] It is also possible that his political and other priorities might not have allowed him the time to go into philosophical speculation. But the fact remains that his appearances in public meetings became fewer

Though the demise of his wife in 1935 might have pulled down his public life, he had also launched himself on a serious research subject: Who were the untouchables? and why had they become untouchables? Why did the caste Hindus treat them in the inhuman fashion that had persisted down to the present day and threatened to go on for ever unless something was done about it? Questions like this must have tormented Ambedkar for many years, but it was not till 1938, that he was able to take time off from his work for the Depressed Classes and start committing the results of his investigations to paper. In March that year, when it seemed there was speculation as to why Dr. Ambedkar had been less conspicuous on public platforms of late and why he was not devoting as much time as usual to the work of Bombay Legislative Assembly, there appeared in the *Bombay Chronicle* an article that showed that the rising untouchable leader had not been passing his time in idleness. *Volume that will Create Consternation among Orthodox and House Reformers,* ran the headline, *Dr. Ambedkar's Forthcoming Magnum Opus.*[60]

This research kept him busy till 1948, and while this *Magnum Opus* never appeared as a whole unit, but sections of this research appeared as separate units or monographs: (1) *What Congress and Gandhi have done to the Untouchables* (1945), (2) *The Untouchables* (1948), (3) *Revolution and Counter Revolution* (which was ready only at the time of Ambedkar's death), and (4) *Riddles of Hinduism.*[61] This research consumed two decades of his time after his Yeola Declaration. During this time he had also involved more deeply in politics, joining the Nehru's Cabinet, and drafting the Constitution of India. But his political career as noted earlier began to set after the debacle of his cherished 'Hindu Code Bill' and his subsequent resignation from the Nehru's Cabinet and finally his defeat in the General Elections of 1952. His election to the Rajya Sabha was a considerably smaller responsibility and he dealt with it with ease till his death.

In addition to all these, Ambedkar was travelling constantly abroad specially after 1950, to study Buddhism in depth and to participate in various Buddhist International Conferences. Thus we see that he had so much to do and the change of religion, which was a very serious matter and he took maximum time to decide, though it appears even before Yeola Declaration his mind was tilted towards Buddhism.

PERSUATIONS

1. From Islam

While the Hindu leaders within and outside the Congress circle tried to convince Ambedkar not to leave the fold of Hinduism, the other minority communities wooed him to their folds. To quote Sangarakshita: "K.L. Gauba, a Muslim leader, telegraphed Ambedkar saying that the whole of Muslim India was ready to welcome and honour him and the untouchables and promising full political, social, economic and religious rights. Other Muslim leaders were no less pressing, and one of them—later reported to have been then the Nizam of Hyderabad (probably the then 'Richest man of the world')—offered Ambedkar the sum of forty or fifty million rupees, if he would undertake to convert the whole untouchable community to Islam..."[62] Paradkar notes: "After the 1935 Yeola resolution to quit 2Hinduism, Muslim leaders welcomed Ambedkar to join Islam. A rumour was once spread that Ambedkar was to join Islam. But Ambedkar denied this. He rejected Islam saying that the Indian Muslims did not take to social reorganisation and were therefore unlike the progressive Muslims under Kamal Pasha of Turkey. The Islamic section of India, because of its fanatically religious spirit, felt the irresistable constraint of a separate national feeling...The problem of the Depressed Classes was to find a solution along lines which would preserve their national homogenity with India. 'One may well ask', he declared if there is any social evil which is found among Hindus and is not found among Muslims?... No words can adequately express the many evils of polygamy, and concubinage and especially as a source of misery to Muslim women...Regarding slavery nothing needs to be said...there is nothing whatever in Islam that leads to the abolition of this curse...As for caste (there is) enough to show that the Mohammedans observe not only caste but also untouchability. Ambedkar's conclusion is: "There can be no manner of doubt that the Muslim society in India is afflicted by the same social evils as afflict the Hindu Society. Indeed Muslims have all the social evils of the Hindus and something more. That something more is the compulsory system of Purdah for Muslim women. ...There is a stagnation not only in the social life but also in the political life of the Muslim community in India. The Muslim have no interest in politics as such. Their predominant interest is religion".[63] We notice something more to this, his intense cultural nationalism. He rejected Islam as well as Christianity because by embracing these religions, he thought, the Scheduled Caste will not only go out of the Hindu religion but also out of Hindu culture. Further, *The Times of India* published Ambedkar's opinion on 24th July 1936: "Conversion to Islam or Christianity will denationalize the Depressed Classes. If they go over to Islam, the number of Muslims will be double and danger of Muslim domination also becomes real. If they go over to Christianity, the numerical strength of the Christians becomes five to six crores. It will help to strengthen to the hold of Britain on the country..."[64] With these reasons, Ambedkar rejected Islam (and Christianity as well).

2. From Christianity

The passage mentioned above is a pointer as to why Ambedkar rejected Christianity. Further, though he was familiar with the Christian tenets, mainly because of his sojourn abroad, and his closeness to Bishop Waskam Picket of the Methodist Church. The invitation to join the Christian faith was not direct at all. Bishop Badley of the Methodist Church said in his response to Ambedkar's Yeola Declaration: "communities consisting of millions of people could become Christians only if members experienced a real change of heart. It was a change of heart that constituted conversions. At the same time he added, Ambedkar's statement would be welcomed by the Christian Church, since it indicated that the Depressed Classes were ambitious for better things in life and that a new era was about to dawn for them".[65]

Christianity practiced in India was, we may boldly say, mostly deplorable and contrary to the tenets of the Gospel of Christ. As early as December 31, 1937, Ambedkar revealed his opinion in a speech to Indian Christians at Sholapur. From his study of comparative religions, he would say that two personalities could captivate him, one of whom was Christ. He told the Christians that their co-religionists in Southern India observed caste in churches. Besides they lagged behind politically. If the Mahar boys became Christians they lost their scholarships. Thus there was no economic gain in their becoming Christians. The Indian Christians, he remarked, never fought for the removal of social injustice.

In August 1944 at Madras, Ambedkar was handed a memorandum from the Tamil Nadu Depressed Classes Association. It stated that conversion to Christianity had not altered their economic and social position. It alleged that former caste Hindus, maintained caste after conversion and ill-treated the Depressed Class Christians. It charged that the Christian missionaries acquiesced caste attitudes among Christians. The memorandum appealed to Ambedkar to deliver "the out-caste Christians from the caste Christians".[66]

During those years Ambedkar believed that his teachings of Christ and the liberation message of St. Paul proved a 'perfect antidote to the poison, injected into our souls and a dynamic, strong enough to lift us out of our present degraded position'. But the Missions here produced 'a different feeling.[67] He saw the Christian Missions in Western India as an instrument of desocialisation, as conversion to Christianity was making Christians of outcaste origin 'selfish and self-centred'.

3. From Sikhism

Probably, the religion he deliberated most to embrace from within was Sikhism before taking a final decision to embrace Buddhism. The following excerpts from Paradkar will do well to explain why. "Sardar Dalip Singh Doabia, Vice President of the Golden Temple Managing Committee, wrote to Ambedkar saying that Sikhism fulfilled the requirements regarding what Ambedkar hoped for conversion. The Sikh-Religion is monotheistic and all loving and provides for equal treatment of all its adherents.[68] Ambedkar said that he wanted to absorb his people into some powerful community and that he was thinking of Sikhism. On January 13, 1936 he attended a Sikh Bhajan with Dr. Solanki. In mid April 1936, he went to attend the Sikh Mission Conference. The conference was well attended by Sikhs and Depressed Class people from the Punjab, Kerala, U.P. and C.P. (now M.P.). The Sikh leaders stressed in their speeches the need for missionary and uplift work among Depressed Classes. Ambedkar replied that he approved the principles of equality, but had not made up his mind which religion to follow... Ambedkar made a positive gesture by sending his son and nephew to the (Sikh) Gurudwara Mandir in Amritsar.

Ambedkar made a statement, reported in the Press (*Times of India*, July 24, 1936), explaining his preference for Sikhism: "Looking at these alternative faiths purely from the standpoint of Hindus, which is the best—Islam, Christianity or Sikhism? Obviously, Sikhism is the best. If the Depressed Classes join Islam or Christianity, they not only go out of Hindu religion, but they also go out of the Hindu culture. On the other hand, if they become Sikhs, they remain within the Hindu culture. This is by no means a small advantage to the Hindus...Conversion to Islam or Christianity will denationalise the Depressed Classes...On the other hand, if they embrace Sikhism, they will not harm the destiny of the country, but they will help the destiny of the country. They will not be denationalised. On the contrary, they will be a help in the political advancement of the country. Thus it is in the interest of the country that the Depressed Classes, if they are to change their faith should go on to Sikhism...The move for conversion to Sikhism has been approved by a number of prominent Hindus, including Sankaracharya...In fact, it is they who took the initiative and pressed it on to me. If I have gone to the length of considering it as an alternative, it is because, I felt a certain amount of responsibility for the fate of the Hindus. ...The Hindu leaders approved the proposal because they believed that Sikhism was a 'branch of Hinduism owing the same culture and principles'. As Ambedkar had reached a measure of rapport with Sikh religious leaders he took another step in the direction of Sikhism and on the 18th September 1936, he sent thirteen men to Sikh Mission at Amritsar to study Sikhism".[69] Dr. Presler notes that "The thirteen were so pripitious as to go over to Sikhism without consulting their leader; he received them coldly on their return...What seems to have turned his mind away from Sikhism was the question of seats for the Depressed Classes should they become Sikhs. Sikhs were granted such seats only in Punjab, his people would actually lose political privileges in other provinces by adopting this religion. Twenty years later he stated in the Parliament that Sikhs are, after all, considered to be Hindus for purposes of law".[70]

We cannot assert that Ambedkar rejected Sikhism as an alternative religion in the sense he rejected Islam and Christianity. 1937 onwards, as we had noted earlier, he was deeply involved in research as to find the origin of untouchables. In the course of the research he came to the conclusion, that the untouchables were originally,—what the sociologists would call—the Broken men and they stuck to Buddhism, the religion of their times and untouchability was imposed on them for sticking on to Buddhism. This imposition was consequent to the revival of Brahminism.

Therefore, it is possible that he being a lineage of 'the Broken men', who later were to become untouchables and identified as Depressed Classes ultimately, his mind certainly was more tilted in favour of Buddhism. There is no evidence of Ambedkar giving serious thought to Sikhism as such in the subsequent years.

Though we would not know if there is any invitation from the Jains to join, Ambedkar had this to say on Jainism: "it was not a powerful religion and that the Ahimsa preached by Jainism was extreme and thus unacceptable"[71].

4. From Buddhism

Though we know that Ambedkar became a Buddhist eventually, we must analyse why he chose Buddhism of all the possibilities. What appears peripherally is that he, having declared that he will not die a Hindu though born as one, he then contemplated about the alternatives. What is to be known for sure that his inclination towards Buddhism has been preceding his declaration at Yeola in 1935.

Alongwith invitations from leaders of other religions, an invitation to join the Buddhist fold also came from the Buddhists. "While the Burmese monk U Ottama... condemned the renunciation of Hinduism by the untouchables, representatives of the Buddhists of Burma, Siam, Tibet and China, who were assembled in Calcutta after the Yeola Conference welcomed Ambedkar's decision and sent him a telegram inviting him to join the Buddhist community. The Secretary of the Mahabodhi Society, Saranath, also sent a telegram. This read, "shocked very much to read your decision to renounce Hindu religion. Very sorry to read your resolution that Depressed Classes should break away completely from Hindu fold. Please reconsider your decision. I see untouchability is being brought to an end by thoughtful Sanatanists themselves. But if you still persist in embracing another religion, you and your community are most cordially welcome to embrace Buddhism which is professed by the greater part of Asia. Among Buddhists there are no religious or social disabilities. We grant equal status to all converts. There are no caste distinctions amongst us. We are willing to send workers".[72] Sangharakshita sardonically comments: "What Ambedkar thought of the telegram is not known, but he could hardly be blamed for thinking that the Mahabodhi Society would not be sorry if he did not 'persist' in embracing any other religion"[73]. What strikes is this: While we see Ambedkar replying to the invitation of leaders of the religion of Islam, Christianity and Sikhism, why is it that Ambedkar did not utter in the affirmative or in the negative in response? Would it not be that Ambedkar took the invitation rather too seriously?

When did Ambedkar's mind get set on Buddhism? Did it begin when Ambedkar was presented with a book on 'Buddha' in 1908 when he passed his Matriculation Examination? If we call it 'providence', had Ambedkar been alive, he would have flatly denied it. (Later on he was to say that he became a Buddhist in his heart when he was 16.) He is said to have read it many times, a voracious reader that he was. Sangharakshita reads between the lines of what Ambedkar wrote as a review article on Bertrand Russell's *The Principles of Social Reconstruction* and mentions that Ambedkar's review is reminiscent of Buddhism's 'Virya' (energy).[74] Later referring to the incident of the burning of *Manusmriti.* He quotes Ambedkar to have exhorted his fellow Mahars that "No lasting progress can be achieved unless we put ourselves through a three-fold process of purification. We must improve the general tones of our behaviour, re-tune our utterance, and revitalize our thoughts"[75]. The three-fold purification of which Ambedkar spoke was, of course, the purification of the three principles of body, speech and mind, which between them make up the individual human being. What is especially noteworthy about Ambedkar's insistance on the need for a three-fold purification, is that whereas references to a three-fold purification, corresponding to a three-fold division of the individual being, are found throughout Buddhist literature, they appear to be unknown to Vedic and pre-Vedic literature of Hinduism.

This suggests that even before the time of the Chowdar Tank campaign, Ambedkar had not only familiarised himself with the Buddhist scriptures, but had started thinking in specifically Buddhist terms. It also suggests, that he saw progress not as simply material but as having a moral and spiritual basis...It certainly indicates a very clear possibility of Ambedkar having an adequate knowledge of Buddhism even before 1927.

Further the incident which Sangharakshita states strengthens Ambedkar's certain knowledge on Buddhism. It also points to the awe he had for Buddhist tradition in that "two days after the burning of *Manusmriti* Ambedkar and his entourage went on an expedition to a place in the neighbourhood of Mahad in order to see the excavation of some ruins that were believed to date from the time of the Buddha. Deeply moved by the sight of the sculptures that had been unearthed, Ambedkar described to his entourage how the Buddha's disciples had lived lives of poverty and chastity and selflessly devoted themselves to the service of the community. In a reverential mood, he asked them not to sit on the ancient stone benches that formed part of the ruins since they may have been the seats of the Buddhist monks"[76] Ambedkar was a 'bookworm' throughout his life, his magnificent collection of books were housed in 'Rajagraha' and he must have been reading in depth on Buddhism, despite his busy schedule. Between 1929 and 1935, which were the crucial years in deciding 'To be or not to be a Hindu'. He had witnessed violent reaction to his attempts to assert human rights for the Depressed Classes. Then he took a decision positively, firmly emphatically and once and for all to leave Hinduism.

During the next few years that followed, he thought not merely of a religion of his choice—which would be Buddhism, considering his dissatisfaction over Sikhism, Islam and Christianity and his inclination towards Buddhism—but though of a religion which would be of great utility value for the ignorant masses of the Mahar community. He studied thoroughly probably till 1950 the *summun bonum* of Buddhism and then decided to embrace Buddhism. What began as a basic look out for mundane benefits of emancipation and amelioration of the Mahars by embracing a new religion—leaving Hinduism—ended in Buddhism as the culmination of a spiritual quest and supramental odyssey. He wanted to posit a religion to his followers that would do good to them and to him collectively. During the momentous period of nearly ten years till his *The Untouchables* come out.

"That the 'untouchables' were originally Buddhists represented a discovery of his own spiritual roots".[77] Preceding this book came his (highly controversial and polemical) *What Gandhi and Congress had done to the untouchables,* which basically was a research work and kept a portion of this work to vent a tirade against Gandhiji and the Congress. 1948 to 1950, we could call as formative years for him to ultimately decide on 'Buddhism' as his future way of life et al.

We should note that Ambedkar concluded his speech to the Mahars in May 1937, by quoting the Buddha; in August 1937, addressing the Depressed Classes at Bombay by quoting the Buddha; in January 1938 he told his gathering at Sholapur that two personalities could captivate him: One was the Buddha and the other was Christ. Thus we see the message of the Buddha has gone too deep into his heart. We have noted earlier that from 1938, his keen intellect was absorbed in the research work on the origin of 'untouchables', which also brought out the antiquity of Buddhism to the core and fore. Sangharakshita says, "In

February 1940 he told the representative of a Bombay newspaper that untouchability was originally imposed as a punishment for sticking to Buddhism when others had deserted it— a thesis he was to develop in his book *The Untouchables* published in 1948"[78]. Five years after the Yeola Declaration he made this statement to the newspaper correspondent; and still eight years later his thesis was developed and found the form of a book.

During these years was not Ambedkar leaning towards Buddhism. Further "In November 1945, the pandal in which Ambedkar addressed the provincial Council Conference of the Scheduled Caste Federation, held in Ahmedabad on the banks of the river Sabarmati, was called Buddhanagar or city of Buddha." While in June the following year he himself gave the college that the people's Education Society had started in Bombay, the name of Siddharth College (Siddhartha being the personal name of the Buddha). What was perhaps of greater significance is that in 1948 he brought out a new edition of P. Lakshminarasu's, *The Essentials of Buddhism,* originally published in 1907...he revealed that he was himself working on a life of the Buddha, in which he intended to deal with some of the criticisms that had been levelled against the teachings of the Buddha by his adversaries—past and present. This life of the Buddha must have been the work that was eventually published under the title *The Buddha and His Dhamma*, and the fact that Ambedkar was engaged on it while still a member of the Union Cabinet showed that he was more preoccupied with Buddhism than ever. He had been making a close study of the Vinaya Pitaka, and it was no doubt partly as a result of this study of the Buddhist Scriptures that he was definitely inclined to Buddhism and had, in fact, more or less made up his mind to embrace that religion. Later in 1950 he told a reporter that he was on his way to embrace Buddhism.[79]

Ambedkar's article on 'Buddha and the future of his religion' appeared in the May 1950 issue of the *Mahabodhi*

Journal. He went to Colombo the same month, the purpose of which was to observe the rituals and ceremonies of Buddhism. There he exhorted the Buddhists to propagate their religion. He addressed the Buddhist youth on 'The Rise and Fall of Buddhism in India'. He also urged the Buddhists of Ceylon to accept the untouchables and look after their interests. In May 1951 his article 'The Rise and Fall of Hindu Women' was published in *Mahabodhi Journal*.

It had been noted that after successfully getting the Constitution of India passed by the Parliament in September 1951, and the rejection of the Hindu Code Bill Ambedkar resigned from Nehru's Cabinet. He was now a freer man to devote his time more to the cause of Buddhism. When he lost his election for the Lok Sabha, he had much more time for Buddhism. In May 1954, he attended the Vaisakha celebrations in Burma and in June he announced that he was going to start a seminary for Buddhist novitiates at Bangalore: In December he was again in Burma, attending the World Fellowship of Buddhists at Rangoon and then went to Mandalay. According to one account that it was here he announced that he and his followers would formally embrace Buddhism in the 2500th year of the Buddhist era, i.e., in 1956-57.

On 25th December 1955, Ambedkar installed the image of the Buddha at Poona. As for his personal intentions, he would dedicate himself to the propagation of the Buddhist faith in India. At that time he was writing a book explaining the tenets of Buddhism in simple language for the benefit of common man. He thought that, when it was finished he would embrace Buddhism.[80]

The book, *Buddha And His Dhamma* was finished by February 1956 and it was given for printing. Finally as promised, he embraced Buddhism along with his wife and followers in October 1956 at Nagpur. The conversion event needs a more elaborate description. Before that we should see what Dr. Ambedkar saw in Buddhism as unique, those which were found wanting in other religions.

Ambedkar was a rationalist and therefore revealed religions did not appeal to him at all. But he emphasised that, "He preferred Buddhism, because it gave three principles in combination which no other religion gave. Buddhism teaches *Pragna* (understanding), *Karuna* (compassion) and *Samatha* (equality). He preferred Buddhism because, like Christianity, it affords hope to the down trodden. He felt that Buddhist Dhamma was more democratic, ethical and egalitarian and hence the inevitable choice.[81] Buddhism obviously is based on reason. There is an element of flexibility inherent in it which is not found in any other religion.[82] In nutshell, Ambedkar found in Buddhism every answer to the question a rational mind may put. Other religions for him were either unpractical and unethical for communal harmony (like Islam), or the followers do not practice the tenets of the founder (like Christianity). As theistic religions believe in God who created all that is on the earth, the logical corollary would be that "he created the stone in the bladder too which did not appeal to the rational man today".[83]

Dr. Presler has other reasons to say in this context: "...there were in him four personal traits that made his choice of Buddhism likely, namely, his negativism, his materialism, his nationalism and his social concern".[84] As we know Hinayana Buddhism is negative towards many established beliefs and practices ... No God, no soul, no immorality, no desire, no attachments, etc. The ability to debunk established norms proved captivating to Ambedkar ... He was anti-Philanthropists, anti-Congress Party, anti-labour unions, anti-Marxist, anti-priests, anti-Gandhi, anti-Civil Disobedience Movement, anti-homeland, anti-contemporary religions, anti-scriptures, anti-democracy at times, anti-the name Harijan, anti-village life, anti-west, and even in an outburst of anger, anti-the Constitution which he helped to write. Temperamentally negative, he was charmed by the negativism of Buddhism (though Dr. Presler's analysis sounds iconoclastic and exaggerated, yet there is a rudiment of truth by and large). Secondly, Dr. Presler says, he was disposed to Buddhism by his materialism and goes on to quote Dr. Ambedkar "It is the duty of the legislature to provide for you food, clothes, shelter, education, medicine, and all the means of earning a livelihood. It is your duty to divert your attention from fasts, worship, penances, and to apply it to capturing law making power. That way lies your salvation. That way will end your starvation". Ambedkar defined religion as "something that offered material prosperity first in this world".[85] On September 28, 1932, he advised his followers to "care more for material good than spiritual food".[86] In closing this paragraph, Dr. Presler says that it seemed to Ambedkar an easy matter to move his materialism into Hinayana Buddhism which appeared to discount the next world.[87]

Dr. Presler's observations on Ambedkar's nationalism and social concern need not be discussed at all, for they stand out for unanimous verdict as 'par excellence' to any reader.

To sum up, Dr. Ambedkar's option for Buddhism was both spiritually and materially motivated, as far as the Mahars and other Depressed Classes were concerned. As for himself, it was basically a thirst for knowledge and research, which made him to conclude that he was of 'Broken men' stock, who were once Buddhists, and who did not give up Buddhism even under torturous emotional persecution and he, might have felt convinced to stick to his 'ancestral' religion. His leadership of the Depressed Masses was undoubtedly vicarious. He said, "For me, personally, there is no bar. If I continue to remain an untouchable, I can attain any position, that a Hindu can...But it is for your emancipation and advancement that conversion appears to be very necessary to me. ... I have to start conversion to improve your lot ..."[88] Yet, towards the end of his study, he was convinced of the validity of Buddha. His final declaration on Buddhism was: the only way!

THE CONVERSION

The event of final decision and the conversion ceremony does not come up merely for an academic exercise. The generally fast working Dr. Ambedkar, was rather too slow to arrive at a decision to embrace Buddhism. Spiritual matters obviously cannot be taken lightly and decided hastily. Dr. Ambedkar's treatment of the subject of conversion which began in 1935 (or may be 1929) and which ended in 1956 reminds one of the old adage, 'Slow and steady wins the race'.

Some of the questions that were in the mind of Dr. 2Ambedkar were where, when and how to adopt Buddhism in a ceremony and having publicly denounced Hinduism two decades ago, how to renounce that publicly. He might have sought the advice of many, but one whom he confided was British born Buddhist monk Sangharakshita who had ministered in India since his youth. In 1954, Ambedkar asked him, if he could administer the 'three refuges' and 'five precepts' at the time of conversion and Sangharakshita suggested the oldest monk in India—U Chandramani. Having decided long ago that the conversion will take place on Vijaya Dasami Day, that day happened to be 14th October in the year 1956, which was also the year of 2500th year of Mahaparinibbana of the Buddha. Regarding the mode, Dr. Ambedkar himself had prepared one, and he also prepared 22 vows to be taken by every Buddhist at the time of initiation ceremony. The venue was thoughtfully chosen to be Nagpur. Some of the Mahars at Poona were given Buddhist Catechism by Sangharakshita as to what it means to be a Buddhist.[89]

On the 13th October Ambedkar convened a press conference to explain his position on conversion. That press conference was by no means a pleasant one. But, one of the most important debate as to what form of Buddhism; his adoption of Buddhism is going to be—Hinayana or Mahayana. Ambedkar declared that his form of Buddhism will be neither Hinayana nor Mahayana, but Navayana (Neo-Buddhism), adopting the actual teachings of the Buddha only. Another important truth which came out during the press conference, was his love for his motherland and his culture: "As for their embracing Buddhism, he had once told Mahatma Gandhi that though he differed from him on the issùe of untouchability, when the time came he would choose only the least harmful way for the country. 'And the greatest benefit I am conferring on the country by embracing Buddhism', he continued proudly, 'for Buddhism is part and parcel of the Bharatiya culture. I have taken care that my conversion will not harm the tradition of culture and history of this land.[90]

OBSTACLES

All things taken care of, Ambedkar had to cross an obstacle but that was to be from his close aides. Even on the 13th October 1956, the day appointed just prior to the date of conversion, some of his close aides suggested that the conversion may please be postponed until after the elections, which were drawing near. This request-knowing pretty well that tens of thousands of the Mahars have come all the way from whereever they may be, and are thronging Nagpur just in response to Ambedkar's call to come and embrace Buddhism—found a fiery response from Dr. Ambedkar. He told them to either embrace Buddhism as originally scheduled, and if they don't decide to embrace Buddhism, they should be prepared to take the consequences and the aides left.[91]

There was yet another problem which was rather technical, and that was that Ambedkar had been totally disillusioned with the Buddhist Sanghas and he had originally decided to take only the first two of the refuges, 'Buddham' and 'Dhammam' but not 'Sangam'. It was Vali Sinha who pointed out that if Ambedkar did not take refuges in the Sangha also, they would not be recognised as Buddhists the world over. To this Dr. Ambedkar finally, though hesitatingly, agreed.

THE DIKSHA BHOOMI AND THE INITIATION

'Diksha Bhoomi', the site of conversion, looked a sea of multitude on the 14th October 1956. At 9:15 a.m. Dr. Ambedkar and his wife took their seats and repeated the three refuges and five precepts. As the time showed 9:45, Dr. Ambedkar was Buddhist now, exactly 21 years after the Yeola Declaration of 13th October 1935, an untouchable then, now emancipated. With him his Brahmin second wife also became a Buddhist. In the olden days of the Buddha and the Sangha also converts were from all castes. As mentioned earlier, Ambedkar had prepared twenty-two vows, which he expected to be taken by every Navayana Buddhist. It is denouncing all that is Hindu, to say the least and emphasising highest ethical and moral conduct and total abstinence. It is recorded by all that when he uttered "I renounce Hinduism", his voice choked with emotion. He was now a Buddhist.

POST INITIATION

Next, Ambedkar did something unusual. Instead of seeking the Buddhist clergy to initiate the 4,00,000 Mahars that had come to take 'Diksha'. Ambedkar himself stood up and administered the oath of three refuges, five precepts and twenty-two vows. Thereby, he introduced the concept of laity taking the right to initiate others into Buddhism and not wait for the clergy's arrival. Within minutes, the Buddhist populace in India had multiplied manifold times.

Next day, i.e., 15th October 1956 Dr. Ambedkar, a nascent Buddhist, came to the same rostrum and addressed a gathering as to what Buddhism means in present day context. In that address he extolled the uniqueness of the Buddha and explained how Buddhism differs from other religions. To conclude that address he exhorted all the new converts (now Buddhists and ex-untouchables) to 'go forth with the message of the Buddha' and to 'go forth to liberate people'.

The entire multitude of people clad in white robes (which they seemed to have secured, some by even selling their ornaments) shouted in unison: "Victory to Lord Buddha: victory to Babasaheb (as he had came to be affectionately called by his followers).

Twenty-one years after the Yeola Declaration, Ambedkar must have heaved a sigh of relief that after conversion he experienced being 'new born' and must have been well content seeing the wave of conversions all over Maharashtra. In his words: "This conversion has given me enormous satisfaction and pleasure unimaginable. I feel as if I have been liberated from hell"[92]...The motive behind the conversion was: "We are making efforts to reach manhood"[93]. As Paradkar says: "It is estimated according to 1961 census, that 15 per cent of India's population—65,000,000 are of Scheduled Class origin. In Nagpur on mass conversion day 2,50,000 people embraced Buddhism. In the State of Maharashtra, Mahars, the upper level outcastes, were the chief ones to follow the example of the 'Saviour' of the untouchables' as the Maharaja of Baroda—Ambedkar's patron at one time — once described him. In various parts of India 30,00,000 embraced Buddhism. How many more of the 65 million would have followed Ambedkar is hard to say".[94] It should be noted that within a period of five years (1956-61), the population of Buddhists registered a spectacular increase of 1670.71 per cent, i.e., from 1,80,823 it rose to 32,50,227. The figures have gone up as the mass conversions initiated by Dr. Ambedkar had been continuing.[95]

THE JOURNEY'S END

It is not often that people *do* what they say. Ambedkar did what he said. It is seldom that people *accomplish* what they wish to *achieve*. Dr. Ambedkar accomplished all that he had wanted to achieve. What remained for him to *do* was to establish a Buddhist fraternity in India to bring back the glory of Buddhism in the days of yore and to weave an international community of Buddhist fellowship. He said a few days before his death: "There was still so much to be done ... So much to be done".[96] Just ten days before his death, Ambedkar attended the fourth conference of the World Fellowship of Buddhists at Kathmandu and returned on the 30th November 1956. He passed away during sleep between the night of 5th and dawn of 6th December 1956 at Delhi. Nehru and other leaders visited his house and transported his mortal remains to Bombay. There the mortal remains of the great son of India and the greatest (ex)untouchable ever was given a great hero's homage by his mourners—longest procession ever witnessed in Bombay. He was cremated at 'Chaitya Bhoomi' at Dadar on 7th December, 1956.

We can say this: The wheel of the Dhamma which the Buddha had set in motion went far and wide, but in India it got stuck. Angarika Dhammapala pulled it out of oblivion and got it set in India for movement again. But Ambedkar set the wheel in motion with a formidable speed and it is still surging forward.

REFERENCES

1. St. Mathew 7:7.
2. Kuber, W.N, *B.R. Ambedkar*, Publications Division, Government of India, 1978, p. 15.
3. Sangharakshita, *Ambedkar and Buddhism*, Windherse Publications, Glasgow, 1986, p. 5.
4. Ahir, D.C., *Gandhi and Ambedkar*, p. 9.
5. Ramteke, Dr. D.L. *Revival of Buddhism in Modern India*, New Delhi, Deep & Deep Publications, 1983, p. 94.
6. Amar Chitra Katha, *Baba Saheb Ambedkar*, India Book House, 1979, p. 19.
7. Kuber, W.N. *op. cit.*, p. 74.
8. *Ibid.*, p. 17.
9. Ramteke, D.L., *op. cit.*, p. 77.
10. *Ibid.*, pp. 77-78.
11. Kuber, W.N., *op. cit.*, p. 17.
12. Ramteke, D.L., *op. cit.*, p. 78.
13. Kuber, W.N., *op. cit.*, p. 18.
14. Ramteke, D.L., *op. cit.*, p. 95.
15. Kuber, W.N., *op. cit.*, p. 18.
16. Ramteke, D.L., *op. cit.*, p. 78.
17. *Ibid.*, p. 78.
18. Kuber, W.N., *op. cit.*, p. 8.
19. *Ibid.*, p. 8.
20. Ramteke, D.L., *op. cit.*, p. 78.
21. Ramteke, D.L., *op. cit.*, pp. 94-95.
22. Vijayakumar, W.R., *op. cit.*, p. 18.
23. Kuber, W.N., *op. cit.*, pp. 22-23.
24. Cf. Ramteke, D.L., *op. cit.*, pp. 98-99.
25. Kuber, W.N., *op. cit.*, pp. 19-20.
26. Ramteke, D.L., *op. cit.*, p. 56.
27. Kuber, W.N., *op. cit.*, p. 25.
28. *Ibid.*, p. 29.
29. Cf. Ahir, D.C., *op. cit.*, pp. 44-45.
30. Ramteke, D.L., *Revival of Buddhism in Modern India*, p. 98.
31. *Ibid.*, p. 99.
32. *Ibid.*, p. 100.

33. *Ibid.*, pp. 100-01.
34. *Ibid.*, p. 101.
35. *Ibid.*, p. 102.
36. Kuber, W.N., *op. cit.*, p. 39.
37. Ahir, D.C., *op. cit.*, p. 55.
38. Cf. Ramteke, D.L., *op. cit.*, pp. 103-04.
39. *Ibid.*, pp. 105-06.
40. *Ibid.*, pp. 106-07.
41. Vijayakumar, W.R., *op. cit.*, p. 22.
42. Ahir, D.C., *op. cit.*, p. 35.
43. Amar Chitra Katha, *Baba Saheb Ambedkar*, India Book House, 1979, p. 32.
44. Presler, Dr. H.H., *India Cultures Quarterly*, Quarter Four, Jabalpur, 1964, p. 9.
45. Ramteke, D.L., *op. cit.*, p. 155.
46. *Ibid.*, pp. 121-22.
47. Vijayakumar, W.R., *op. cit.*, p. 28.
48. Ramteke, D.L., *op. cit.*, p. 122.
49. Vijayakumar, W.R., *op. cit.*, p. 30.
50. *Ibid.*, p. 30.
51. *Ibid.*, p. 30.
52. Ibid., *op. cit.*, p. 39.
53. Ramteke, D.L., *op. cit.*, p. 122.
54. Sangharakshita, *op. cit.*, pp. 63-64.
55. *Ibid.*, p. 64.
56. Ramteke, Dr. D.L., *op. cit.*, pp. 87-88.
57. *Ibid.*, p. 123.
58. Presler, Dr. H.H., 'The Neo-Buddhist Stir in India', *India Cultures Quarterly*, 1964, Quarter Four, p. 6.
59. Sangharakshita, *op. cit.*, p. 58.
60. *Ibid.*, pp. 81-82.
61. *Ibid.*, pp. 82-83.
62. *Ibid.*, p. 61.
63. Paradkar, B.A.M., 'The Religious Quest of Ambedkar', *Ambedkar and the Neo-Buddhist Movement*, pp. 52-55.
64. Presler, Dr. H.H., *op. cit.*, p. 11.
65. Sangharakshita, *op. cit.*, pp. 61-62.
66. Presler, Dr. H.H., *op. cit.*, p. 10.

67. Cf. Paradkar, B.A.M., *Ambedkar and the Neo-Buddhist Movement,* pp. 59-61.
68. Cf. Presler, *op. cit.*, p. 10.
69. Paradkar, B.A.M., *op. cit.*, pp. 53-57.
70. Presler, *op. cit.*, p. 11.
71. Paradkar, B.A.M., *op. cit.*, p. 58.
72. Sangharakshita, *op. cit.*, p. 62.
73. *Ibid.*, pp. 62-63.
74. *Ibid*, pp. 52-53.
75. Sangharakshita, *op. cit.*, p. 56.
76. *Ibid.*, *op. cit.*, p. 58.
77. *Ibid.*, *op. cit.*, p. 94.
78. *Ibid.*, *op. cit.*, p. 69.
79. Cf. *Ibid.*, pp. 71-73.
80. Cf. Sangharakshita, *op. cit.*, pp. 76-77.
81. Cf. Kuber, *B.R. Ambedkar*, pp. 84-88.
82. Paradkar, B.A.M., *op. cit.*, p. 64.
83. *Ibid.*, p. 64.
84. Presler, Dr. H. H., *op. cit.*, pp. 12-14.
85. *Ibid.*, pp. 12-14.
86. *Ibid.*,
87. *Ibid.*,
88. Sangharakshita, *op. cit.*, pp. 65-66.
89. *Ibid.*, *op. cit.*, p. 20.
90. *Ibid.*, *op. cit.*, p. 132.
91. *Ibid.*, *op. cit.*, pp. 133-34.
92. Paradkar, B.A.M., *op. cit.*, p. 61.
93. *Ibid.*,
94. *Ibid.*, p. 66.
95. Cf. Ahir, D.C., *Buddhism in Modern India*, p. 38.
96. *Ibid.*, p. 38.

4

NEO-BUDDHISM AS A SOCIAL PHILOSOPHY

THE NATURE OF NEO-BUDDHISM

The followers of Neo-Buddhism—the Neo-Buddhists, to begin with, were en masse converts following the footsteps of one man (Dr. Ambedkar) who was the only one among the lakhs belonging to his community—to know for sure which religion he is embracing and why. The rest—majority being illiterates—would they know the rational superiority or otherwise of their ancestral religion *vis-a-vis* Buddhism? The answer would appear to be an emphatic 'No'. Therefore, one may raise a genuine question: Does the mass conversion imply blind faith in the path of the Buddha or blind faith in their leader who had told them that Buddhism is the way? This is a very sensitive question for study and analysis.

While analysing 'Neo-Buddhism' as a social philosophy, one has to try and determine the nature of 'Neo-Buddhism' as a sub-sect of Buddhism itself, more so, as a way of life in today's context. Is it one of the modern religious movements or as Dr. Presler would call it: "a Neo-Buddhist mass deeply stirred"?[1] If Neo-Buddhism is indeed how Dr. Presler perceived it, then it would have been an inconsequential sporadic movement which should have withered by now. But as posterity had been witnessing, it may be asserted that it is: (a) a dynamic force; (b) a religious movement based on socio-economic and ethical principles; and (c) a catalyst for the well-being of the down-trodden.

A DYNAMIC FORCE

It won't be an exaggeration to say that Dr. Ambedkar and Neo-Buddhism are synonymous. When Ambedkar returned from the USA he plunged mainly into alleviation of the untouchable communities as a whole—not only his own community (the Mahars) exclusively. Therefore, in all his activities, he had the solidarity of all the untouchables from all over the country. After Yeola Declaration, outcastes were re-christened Harijans by Gandhiji in his effort to obliterate untouchability and under his guidance many outcastes,—Babu Jagjivan Ram, the foremost among them—opted to remain within the Hindu fold. But one outcaste community—Mahars, to which Ambedkar belonged—was solidly behind him for whatever he said or did. He had a sway over them. It was a blind hero-worship. When he finally decided to embrace Buddhism, only the Mahar community—illiterates, the gullible were with him in toto. Even among the Mahars, some of his own semi-literate lieutenants tried to dissuade him from taking Diksha on the scheduled day. But the mass conversion in 1956 was virtually a blind faith reposed in Dr. Ambedkar by the Mahars, without knowing anything deeply about the religious tenets of Buddhism. It was the British monk Sangharakshita who addressed a gathering of 3000 untouchables at Worli (Bombay) on the 1st of January 1956 (by prior arrangement by Dr. Ambedkar) and imparted basic catechism on Buddhism—"What it means to become a Buddhist".[2]

For Ambedkar, Buddhism had given him in his own words: "enormous satisfaction and pleasure unimaginable". Quite true for a rationalist like Dr. Ambedkar, a religion like Buddhism must appeal. He was advising his fellow Mahars to embrace it for the sociological utility value of Buddhism and for its spiritual demands. Though he said, "I do not want any blind followers. I do not like sheep mentality",[3] how could he have realised, or how could he have expected illiterates under social subjugation and miserable environment, to overnight grasp the depth of Buddhist tenets and accept them by faith? But the vast majority of the Mahars who took the initiation, did so, because they had immense faith in their beloved leader. Dr. Ambedkar told them on the eve of great conversion that Buddhism "is the best religion in the world and there can be absolutely no doubt about it,"[4] "this path leads to progress"[5] "Buddhism is the only religion which does not recognise caste and affords full scope for progress"[6]. "If we have any hope it is by renouncing Hinduism and following the path of the Buddha"[7] and "those who wish to come under the refuge of Buddha should do so after counting the cost, for it is a religion very difficult to practice"[8]. Could it be that the esoteric truth of Buddhism as an answer to the sociological problems of the Mahars were understood *ad verbatim* by those hundreds of thousands who became Buddhists on 15th October 1956 and lakhs of people thereafter, or, is it a response to what Dr. Ambedkar said on the same day to those initiated namely, " All I wish today is that you should have faith in me and follow me"[9]. The first converts at Nagpur mostly were untaught on the principal tenets of Buddhism. Therefore we may state that unlike the first sermon of the Buddha at Saranath when he convinced the five disciples by penetrative discourse, the first ever mass conversion—was childlike faith in Buddhism. This 'faith in Buddhism' is the corollary of the unshakeable faith in the leadership of Dr. Ambedkar. The rational analysis and conviction were left to be pondered by the posterity—the second generation onwards. This faith was consequent to the struggle for self-respect, social equality and justice which the untouchables had been fighting for (by peaceful means) for the past three decades under Dr. Ambedkar. The culmination of this struggle was in renouncing Hinduism and embracing Buddhism.

Dr. Ambedkar's calls to his fellow Mahars have been always genuine on any socio-political issue, and this call to embrace Buddhism has been due to his firm conviction that Buddhism was the *Only Way*—out of barricades caused for the 'untouchables' by casteism and a way into their prosperity and progress. Thus the first batch of converts, it did not take a long time to realise that to ensure their human dignity, embracing the path of the Buddha was the best thing they could do 'under the circumstances'. In the personal interviews that the author conducted by way of research, this fact was evidenced. One early convert told that if the Buddha was a *mārga dātā* of the world, Baba Saheb was the *mārga dātā* of the Mahars. That is why Ambedkar was eulogised by the outcastes in general and the Mahars in particular.

The second generation who might have been (in 1956) in their lean years—less or around 10, when grew up as Neo-Buddhists realised the wisdom of their parents*. These second generation are fairly well placed in life, by and large. Neo-Buddhism by showing the path to progress and prosperity is not a mere guide-post. It is a dynamic force in the sense it has not let the Mahars to remain static. The

*Written testimonies of these second generation are found later in this study, which point to the fact that they are Buddhists by conviction and that Dr. Ambedkar is the fountain head of their social change and well-being.

dynamism inherent in Neo-Buddhism is rare in the sense that probably this is the first of its kind among religions on the whole that a comprehensive package of economic welfare, social progress, and spiritual satisfaction is seen as its three-fold objectives. The post-Ambedkar period has seen and is seeing that this movement is gathering momentum and spreading far and wide in India. Can socio-economic progress oriented movement can come under the umbrella of conventional or traditional religions? What way is this movement different from purely materialistic movements like communism or syndicalism? To ask a fundamental question, can this be called a religious movement at all? This leads us to analysing if Neo-Buddhism can be well-defined as a religious movement or a religion by itself. As a religious movement is it 'Salvation' oriented? If it is so, 'Salvation' from what? Is it merely a freedom from *karma* and rebirth, which was the starting point of seekers of all Heterodox Systems, having felt the old orthodoxy wanting? These are some of the questions that needs to be discussed vividly. But, there is dynamism inherent in the Neo-Buddhist movement. It is a dynamic force.

A RELIGIOUS MOVEMENT

Dr. Ambedkar's conviction was that where there is no religion, people will perish. This is the conviction of all those who feel the need to have religion as the purpose of their very existence. Deeply religion-conscious than being religious, Dr. Ambedkar wanted to live within the realm of a religion, but a religion that would assure liberty, equality and justice for every adherent. He was no doubt deeply frustrated with the evils of casteism within the framework of Hinduism to begin with, but in course of time this frustration successively turned into rebellion, to condemnation, to denunciation and ultimately, into conversion. He had been educating his fellow outcastes on the evils of casteism from the 20's and drove home time and again that their miserable state and status were consequent to that. He used very violent language to din it into the heads of the outcastes. This continuous onslaught and tirade against casteism and the adamant, hostile attitude of the then high castes prepared the minds of the outcastes—specially the Mahars —more than to denounce Hinduism, to follow what Ambedkar was to do. This went on for three decades.

When Dr. Ambedkar finally announced his decision to embrace Buddhism it was not merely a change of a religion for him but also a change of heart. For nearly four decades Ambedkar had been not only studying the tenets of Buddhism, but participating in the Buddhist meetings at the international level. One may posit that his acceptance of the tenets of Buddhism was rational. His speeches and writings showed evidence of his analytic mind. His *magnum opus* revealed some of his thoughts which were to disturb the minds of all the orthodox Buddhists the world over. His conclusion was that the Theravada or Hinayana Buddhism would not be acceptable as he questioned the "four noble truths" (*Arya Satya*) and many other traditions associated with the life and teachings of the Buddha; nor would the Mahayana Buddhism would be acceptable to him as this would deify the Buddha himself, which was contrary to his conviction.

Generally it is said by many that Dr. Ambedkar was like Moses of the Bible's Old Testament.[10] One can go a step higher and say that in giving Neo-Buddhism to the Mahars and the outcastes Ambedkar was verily like Moses who not only freed his people from bondage, but also taking them out of the land of Egypt into a Mount Sinai and gave them the Ten Commandments. Similarly Dr. Ambedkar took the Mahars out of the caste dominated society and gave them Buddhism in a modified form with twenty-two vows. The purpose of any religion is, first and foremost, spiritual satisfaction. This, Dr. Ambedkar fully admitted.

What is important for us to note is that the second generation onwards and specially from the seventies, they are ardent followers and propagandists. The movement grew over the years even these nigh four decades and is gathering momentum. If this is not a religious movement, it would have just stopped at 'Dr. Ambedkar's Education Society', etc. Instead, what we find in a Buddhist Booklet is true: "Within exactly 52 days of his conversion into Buddhism, Dr. Ambedkar passed away on 6th December, 1956. This was a terrible calamity, but the followers of Dr. Ambedkar faced it with great courage and went ahead with the conversion movement with redoubled vigour. ...The Buddhist Society of India decided to continue the conversion movement and the masses responded to it with an enthusiasm for beyond our expectation... Many conversion ceremonies were held in different parts of India to spread the conversion movement and the following are noteworthy in recent time:

1. The conversion ceremony was held in Bombay on 20th October 1969;
2. Gorakhpur Ceremony on 14th April 1970;
3. The Gazipur Ceremony on 18th April 1970;
4. The Mirzapur Ceremony on 7th May 1970;
5. The Saranath Ceremony on 29th May 1970;
6. The Calcutta Ceremony on 22nd November 1970;
7. The Patna Ceremony on 13th June 1971;
8. The Allahabad Ceremony on 20th November 1971; and
9. The Basti Ceremony on 30th January 1972...."[11]

There have been subsequently many more conversions over the past two decades. The conversion movement is still going on unabated. Even in this decade, "The Deccan Herald of 12th August 1990 reported the conversion of 10 lakh `Harijan's to Buddhism in U.P. What started off at Nagpur on 14th October 1956 could be called a Religious

Fission—breaking up from Hinduism and then on we see a spate of Religious Fusion—converging of many converts into Buddhism all over India. The religious zeal the Neo-Buddhists is evidenced by a single example as we browse through the booklet 'Ambedkar's Patriotic Call'. This booklet begins with a photopicture of a quotation from the Buddha: "Go ye, O Bhikkus, and wander forth for the gain of the many, for the welfare of the many, in compassion for the world..."; followed by the photopicture of Dr. Ambedkar clad in white with a quotation from Dr. Ambedkar himself: "Go forth with the message of the Buddha; Go forth to liberate people".[12] In the same booklet, the objects of the society is found, the fifth of which is "to train workers to carry the message of Buddhism to all parts of India and to establish study circles for the purpose".[13] This points to the missionary zeal of the Neo-Buddhists, which is active even today.

Further, Buddhist Viharas are built with the same enthusiasm wherever possible and plausible. Many stupas and Buddhist memorials have been and are being built. A monumental hemispherical dome to commemorate the mass revival of Buddhism in India has been built at Nagpur at the very site where Dr. Ambedkar and the first mass conversion took place in 1956. Dr. Ambedkar had planned to start a Buddhist Seminary to train monks. This may some day materialise.

Whatever deeds Dr. Ambedkar did they were pragmatic moves and strategic, aimed at the greater happiness of greatest number of persons. His was a movement right through aimed at securing human dignity for the down trodden Mahar mass. Stir is shortlived, but Ambedkar's movement has outlived him. He had the sway and control over his Mahar mass, not taught by politics, but as situation demanded his was a response to the call from within to alleviate the woes of his community at large —the outcastes, and the untouchables.

What is the conclusion? Neo-Buddhism is a strong religious movement, growing stronger with missionary zeal. It is a socio-economic and ethics-oriented religious movement, wherein spiritual bliss and mundane prosperity are interwoven with each other so much, it is difficult to separate one from the other.

A CATALYST FOR THE WELL-BEING OF THE DOWNTRODDEN

The word 'catalyst' is basically a scientific term related to chemical reactions of substances. This word is generally adapted to refer to an ingredient that steps up action in day-to-day use. In the same sense, Neo-Buddhism functions as a 'catalyst' for the well-being of the former outcastes.

Religion in its strict sense refers to belief in supernatural or divine beings. But it also means any specific system of belief, worship, conduct, etc. ... often involving a code of ethics and a philosophy. Though devoid of God, Neo-Buddhism is a religion in the accepted sense of the word. Can a religion play the role of catalyst in the material welfare of its adherents? Buddhism being traditionally understood as world-negating, how can Neo-Buddhism be world-affirming and thus be constituent not only for the spiritual welfare but also for the material welfare too?

Dr. Ambedkar had said that in Buddhism there is an element of flexibility which is not seen in other religions. In the revealed religions spiritual welfare in one's relationship to God is of utmost priority and material welfare is relegated to the rear. What we see in Neo-Buddhism is that one's spiritual satisfaction and bliss are as important as change of social status, economic prosperity, academic progress and political awareness. It is total development of each individual. Equality *(Samta)* was an important concept for Ambedkar as it referred not only to men but to women as well. The purpose of conversion to Buddhism was of course liberation from Hinduism. Also, as Kadam says, "it was down to earth, healthy robust, rational, enlightened, scientific, cultured and humane approach to overcome the problems created by Vedicism, Brahminism and Hinduism, down the ages that made life a misery for the 'untouchables in India'.[14]

1. Change in Social Status

As Neo-Buddhism is certainly down to earth, it would overcome the problems of untouchability leading to social ostracism, gross ignorance, and static, degraded social status. Neo-Buddhism came as an antidote to this sad state of remaining the lowest for ever. In this sense Neo-Buddhism is unique and probably unparalleled in the history of religions.

As noted earlier if Tilak had said that Swaraj was his birthright, Ambedkar said that it was his birthright to lead a human and honourable life. His foremost claim was human dignity which was denied to him even after his return from overseas with many degrees. Having relinquished many good career offers that came, he fought for human honour not only for himself, but for his fellow outcastes. Within the frame of a caste-ridden society, it was all along a struggle —struggle to draw water from the same source point, struggle for temple entry, struggle for equality in education and many others. Some he secured, some not—but whatever he secured was not without struggle. Struggling Ambedkar and his fellow Mahars became ex-untouchables. (We must note that many out-castes of South India embraced Christianity only to get out of this rut.)

The Mahars by becoming Buddhists were not merely out of any caste, but within the framework of a religion which assures equality for all and which is practised by billions all over the world. Theoretically speaking, even if the Mahars were to do menial jobs, as Buddhists they are to be reckoned as beings worth, dignity and honour. It was not merely amelioration nor alleviation nor mitigation but reaching lofty heights of social equality. Sangharakshita writes effectively on this phenomenon of transformation: "speaking at the time of his conversion to Buddhism, Ambedkar declared that he felt as though he had been delivered from hell, and there is not doubt that the hundreds of thousands of untouchables who followed his example felt similarly. The hell from which they had been delivered was the hell of caste, to which they had been condemned for centuries and which had inflicted on them, in the most systematic manner, what Ambedkar himself characterized as torment".[15] Someone had used an allegory to refer to the inner change of a person from worst moral conduct to the best—"from the guttermost to the uttermost". Symbolically, this phrase would do well to refer to the social change of any person from low to high status. Hence when an outcaste became a Buddhist, the social stigma associated with his former caste is theoretically gone just then and there; it may linger till it is obliterated.

What is special about Neo-Buddhism in bringing about this effect? What way is this religious movement different from those of Christianity, or Islam or Sikhism which guarantees equality of all within the concept of Fatherhood of God and the brotherhood of man? The answer would be that not only because these religions are theistic and Neo-Buddhism atheistic but also because these religions demand more loyalty to the faith from its followers; there is no mundane prosperity theologically linked with its growth. Neo-Buddhism, as conceived by Dr. Ambedkar, is all inclusive as mentioned earlier—spiritual satisfaction and mundane prosperity including intellectual growth; in other words, growth within and without.

There is yet another aspect of social status as visualised by Dr. Ambedkar. Long before Women's Liberation Movement came into being, Ambedkar attacked Manu for codifying the social strata in general, but specially for placing the outcastes low. With equal vehemence he attacked Manu for reducing woman to a non-entity. In *The Rise and Fall of Hindu Woman,* he points out that even a Brahmin woman has no status of her own even though the women of ancient times enjoyed high positions as teachers, and as performers of sacrifices. They commanded respect even by a king: He holds Manu's Laws as the cause of woman's degradation. On the contrary, in the same treatise Ambedkar shows how the Buddha was open to the question of women as honourable beings. He points out that since the Buddha allowed women to become Bhikkunis— be they of Brahmin origin or of Shudra. He further writes that virginity was not the criterion for a woman to become a Bhikkuni. He (the Buddha) allowed married, unmarried, even transformed prostitutes to join the Sangha; but once a male or female joins the Sangha strict celebacy was to be maintained. The Bhikkus and the Bhikkunis, of course, could meet, but they would reside separately.

This conviction that male and female are equal socially, made Neo-Buddhists equal not only caste-wise but also sex-wise. The present generation of Neo-Buddhists has amongst its intelligentsia not only men but women as well. Women are not assigned to a closet as in the past. But for Neo-Buddhism their fate would have been the same.

2. Gandhi vis-a-vis Ambedkar

For both Mahatma Gandhi and Ambedkar men and women were equal. Both of them wanted to eradicate untouchability. Instead of both of them taking a position that would be complementary to either of them, their positions differed in achieving their common end of obliteration of untouchability. While Dr. Ambedkar was a champion to the cause of eradication of untouchability, Gandhiji's "Nothing will satisfy Gandhi, till the last vistage of untouchability is eradicated".[16]

The basic difference in both their approaches was casteism itself. Gandhiji wanted the class structure of castes graded as they are traditionally, minus the problem of untouchability. Dr. Ambedkar envisaged a society without any caste barrier. For Ambedkar removal of untouchability was his topmost priority. For Gandhiji, removal of untouchability was one of his many programmes. Gandhiji's attempt was to ennoble any kind of menial work and he christened the outcastes as 'Harijans'. Ambedkar did not like the term at all. He also did not like any patronage on sympathetic or compassionate grounds. His approach was that of a struggle, whereas Gandhiji's was that of reform. It appears that while Gandhiji was an idealist with regards to untouchability, Ambedkar was certainly a practical realist. When he realised this impossibility, he embraced Buddhism and his 'Neo-Buddhism' functions as catalyst for the social well being for the Mahars and the all outcastes.

As noted, after independence, untouchability was reckoned an offence (Cf. Constitution of India, Art. 17). Ambedkar had leaned towards Buddhism and called upon his people to embrace Buddhism. By virtue of leaving Hinduism and embracing a casteless Buddhism, the Mahars got a social status. Gandhiji's efforts had won the untouchables facilities within the Hindu framework.

3. Economic Prosperity

Dr. Ambedkar was a qualified economist. While social equality of the out-castes was his top priority, the economic progress of his community was the juxtaposed next.

The economist in Dr. Ambedkar pondered over as to how he could bring about an economic change for such a community caught in the web of accepted norms of a society. He, as noted earlier, first of all, had *Mahar Watan* abolished. But for a change over from a pre set profession of hereditary to that of choice of the individual, it would not have been possible, had not the Mahars become

Neo-Buddhists. If we find among the Neo-Buddhists scholars, engineers, doctors, businessmen and others today owning bungalows and vehicles, it is because of the conversion of their parents and grandparents.

On the eve of his conversion, he said: "I know myself what sort of hardships the poor have to bear. We must launch our struggle keeping in view the economic aspects and I am not against this idea. We should progress economically too and endeavour to become independent. I have been struggling myself throughout my life to that end. Not only this, I very much desire mankind to become economically strong".[17] Economic progress of the Mahars was one of the main concerns of Dr. Ambedkar. The study of the economics of untouchability warrants a detailed study. For the present it would suffice to state that Neo-Buddhism is a catalyst for the economic prosperity for the Mahars.

4. Academic Progress

Ambedkar had said that knowledge is power and he had that power in abundance. Though he said that "untouchability cannot be removed by education alone",[18] yet he was greatly committed to the cause of education. He founded the People's Education Society of Bombay in July 1945. He started the Siddharth College, Bombay in 1946. Though he was advocating the need of education among his fellow Mahars, that his calls to this cause for decades did not have its desired impact until after the Mahars embracing Neo-Buddhism. The children of those who were the converts along with Dr. Ambedkar in 1956, are an educated lot. If Neo-Buddhism is not a catalyst for education, would the present State of literacy among the Mahars be what it is today?

5. Political Awareness

One of the many teachings of Ambedkar to the Mahars was that they should enter politics and gain power. While he came to national limelight for Mahad Tank episode and other satyagrahas; his controversy at the national level came to be well known when he successfully got separate electorates for the Depressed Classes after the Second Round Table Conference and against which Gandhiji went on fast unto death. As noted earlier, though Ambedkar had to give up what he had secured so as to enable Gandhiji to end his fast, gaining political successes appears to be one of the prime movers for Dr. Ambedkar. In 1932, he formed the Anti-untouchability League which finally came to be known as Harijan Sevak Sangh. He later on became a member of the Bombay Legislative Assembly, formed the Labour Party and finally All India Scheduled Castes Federation. While presiding over the inauguration of the School of Politics, Pune (in August 1945) he commended the study of Politics.

The followers of Ambedkar might have been marvelling at his achievements but there appears to be none who could keep pace with him within his community. However, the present position of the Neo-Buddhists evidence sharp political awareness and acumen. While some of them have taken to politics as a vocation, the vast majority of them are politically conscious of their responsibilities as a citizen. Some of them have opted to remain within the Scheduled Castes, though they are Neo-Buddhists at heart, so that they may contest the elections in the reserved constituencies. By winning the elections, they would render all services they can to promote the interests of the Neo-Buddhists. (This is happening in Maharashtra.) Now, the rise of Bahujan Samaj Party under the leadership of Mr. Kanshi Ram bears testimony to this.

Even the strength and political awareness of the Dalits, specially in the mid India, can be boldly said to be path shown by Dr. Ambedkar. But as far as Neo-Buddhists are concerned— specially those of Mahars of Maharashtra— they have become a politically conscious people. Needless to mention Neo-Buddhism is not only a religious movement but a political mentor too, reminding the Neo-Buddhists the political achievements of Dr. Ambedkar and their utility value for them.

Thus, we may conclude that Neo-Buddhism is a catalyst for political awareness of the Mahars today.

To wind up, we may say that, as a part of the history of religions in India, the contributions of Neo-Buddhism has been significant specially with regard to the Mahars. Now more and more "outcastes and untouchables", Mahars apart, are embracing Neo-Buddhism as a way of life. This religious movement which does not restrict its influence in the spiritual realm only, is helping them to an all-round development in every sphere of life. This is unlike most of the traditional religions. As a heterodox movement perhaps communism is the only movement which caters to the social welfare of its members. Neo-Buddhists are sure that Buddhism is the only antidote to communism. Dr. Ambedkar's vision of the welfare of his community and India on the whole by embracing Buddhism seems fully justified when we see the results of the first mass conversion and the conversions that followed.

REFERENCES

1. Presler, Dr. H.H., *op. cit.*, p. 24.
2. Sangharakshita, *Ambedkar and Buddhism*, p. 20.
3. *Ambedkar's Patriotic Call*, The Buddhist Society of India, Hyderabad, 1978, p. 5.

4. *Ambedkar's Patriotic Call*, The Buddhist Society of India, Hyderabad, 1978, p. 14.
5. *Ibid.*, p. 11.
6. *Ibid.*, p. 10.
7. *Ibid.*, p. 9.
8. *Ibid.*, p. 5.
9. *Ibid.*, p. 15.
10. Cf. Kadam, K.N. (Ed.) *Ambedkar and the Significance of His Movement*, Bombay, Popular Publication, 1991, p. xiii.
11. *Bodhisattva Ambedkar's Patriotic Call*, The Buddhist Society of India, Hyderabad, 1978, pp. 17-18.
12. *Ibid.*, opening pages.
13. *Ibid.*, p. 16.
14. Kadam, K.N., *op. cit.*, p. 47.
15. Sangharakshita, *Ambedkar and Buddhism*, p. 28.
16. Cf. Kadam, K.N. (Ed.), *op. cit.*, p. 100.
17. *Ambedkar's Patriotic Call*, p. 5.
18. *Ibid.*, p. 7.

5

THE SCRIPTURE OF THE NEO-BUDDHISTS

The only literature which could be termed Neo-Buddhist Doctrinal text is Ambedkar's *Buddha and His Dhamma*. Many of his understanding of Buddhism he had written as articles for nearly two decades. Before publicly embracing Buddhism, he assimilated all his thoughts, wrote *Buddha and His Dhamma* in the early fifties despite indifferent health. This constitutes Ambedkar's doctrinal legacy to his Neo-Buddhist followers.

Now for Hinayists or Mahayanists there were oceans of literature and Bhikkus and Bhikkunis spent their life time reading them. Ambedkar's conception of Buddhism was neither Hinayana nor Mahayana. He had an entirely different understanding of Buddhism itself. Hence he reviewed the tenets of Buddhism.

The text indicates a definite mind of Dr. Ambedkar as to the form of Buddhism he and his fellow Mahars would be adopting. It also to provides a concise Buddhist Text like Bible—(should we call it Bhima Pitaka?). It was and is the first and the last religious text on Neo-Buddhist faith. On its publication in 1957, the reaction of Buddhist monks and scholars overseas was varied. One reviewer wrote: "Indeed the whole book explains the hatred and aggressiveness they (the Neo-Buddhists) nourish and display. Ambedkar's Buddhism is based on Hate, the Buddha's on compassion.... The title should be changed from *Buddha and his Dhamma* to that of *Ambedkar and his Dhamma*, for he preaches non-Dharma as Dharma for motives of social and political reform".[1] The other reviewer in the Light of Dharma observed: "Although this was a book by a great man, unfortunately, it was not a great book which the author with all his manifold virtues was not fit to write... the great doctor tampered with the texts and whenever he found views inconvenient to his own, denounced them as later accretions made by monks".[2]

Nearly thirty years after *Buddha and His Dhamma* was published and reviewed, the British monk Mahasthavir Sangharakshita's book *Ambedkar and Buddhism* was published. Sangharakshita had known Dr. Ambedkar personally and he was the only monk who administered Buddhist catechism to the early converts. He has made painstaking and illuminating review. Sangarakshita drives home that *Buddha and His Dhamma* was begun in right earnestness but completed in a hurry: he compares Ambedkar's *magnum opus* with that of Paul Carus's *The Gospel of Buddha*: traces where Ambedkar should have drawn the sources from; and interprets the mind of Ambedkar chapter by chapter. For him the *Buddha and His Dhamma* "was meant for those who were disillusioned with Hinduism... what is more perhaps important still, whereas Carus presents data of the Buddha's life in the light of what he terms its religio-philosophical importance, Ambedkar presents them in the light of what many may be termed its socio-political importance, Ambedkar's approach to Buddhism is social and ethical rather than philosophical and mystical, as even a short account of the *Buddha and His Dhamma* will be sufficient to reveal".[3]

The *Buddha and His Dhamma* can be treated as the religious text of Neo-Buddhism and in it are the Doctrinal tenets. This compendium has assimilated substance of the Buddhist literature devoid of any supernatural or tantric or yogic experiences. Such a text should be acclaimed as an universal authority on Buddhism. Why is it deemed controversial and unacceptable in the orthodox Buddhist world? The answer, first, would that in this work, Ambedkar shakes the very fundamental doctrine of the *Arya Satyas*—the four noble truths. Ambedkar says in the introduction "The four Aryan truths are a great stumbling block in the way of Non-Buddhists accepting the Gospel of Buddhism. For the four Aryan truths make the Gospel of Buddha—a Gospel of Pessimism. Do they form part of the original gospel or are they a later accretion by the monks"?[4] We may note that the four Aryan truths may be a stumbling block for suprarationalists and the supra-realists like Dr. Ambedkar to accept the Gospel. The third of the Aryan truth offers optimism to counter the pessimism of the first. But for a Neo-Buddhist, *Buddha and His Dhamma*—as of today—is infallible.

The other three problems that Ambedkar seeks to solve are:

(1) Buddha's renunciation, (which is 'not taken seriously by Buddhist scholars'[5]), (2) the doctrines of karma and rebirth, and (3) the requisite of Bhikku. These three are disturbing features for any Buddhist monk, while denial of four Aryan Truths are shocking for any Buddhist and `stumbling block' for a non-Buddhist.

We may briefly get acquainted with the subject matter of the textbook—Book I deals with Prince Siddhartha Gautama—his birth to his renunciation, and taking the *Parivraja*, his vast learning and Enlightenment, a New Dhamma, Gautama becoming the Buddha, Buddha's meeting with people and the discourses he had, Buddha's contemporaries and Buddha's attitude towards them. It ends with the philosophical tenets—what he rejected, modified and accepted.

The Second Book(Book II) begins with the chapter 'To preach or not to preach' — a long soliloquy (reminiscing 'To be or not to be' of *Hamlet*). This book is important for, in this, the Buddha equates the 'High and the Holy' with the 'Low and the Lowly', the fallen and the criminals.[6] In this book, the Buddha is portrayed to be diffident about his own ability to preach. One of the important points is the two types of conversion of a Buddhist—first, that of a convert becoming a Bhikku, which demands taking vows under pain of punishment if the vows are breached, and secondly, that of the convert (*upasaka*) remaining a householder, having property, but his rules are precepts, i.e., he is to follow the rules to the best of his ability.[7] The most important aspect of this Book is Ambedkar's re-presentation of the Buddha's first sermon (in the Deer Park at Saranath), where the traditional four noble truths, and the eight-fold path are deftly replaced by Ambedkar's postulates of no-God, no-soul, man to man relationship, objective of the Dhamma being removal of suffering and this objective is achieved by following the path of purity, path of righteousness and the path of virtue.

The Third Book deals with the central doctrines of the Buddha. But what appears to be the square peg in a round hole is Part II of the Book, namely,—"what others understood him (Buddha) to have taught". Raising the possible questions which are philosophical in nature, Ambedkar springs modern questions like "Did Buddha teach justice, love, liberty, equality, fraternity?" and asks a last question "Could Buddha answer Karl Marx?" Ambedkar asserts all these questions and concludes saying that the Buddha has a social message. He goes on to say that Buddha had a different classification and explains vividly those classifications—*Dhamma, Adhamma* and *Saddhama*. In the succeeding chapters, we find that Dhamma is to maintain purity of life, to reach perfection in life, to live in *Nibbana*, to give up craving, to believe that all compound things are impermanent, and to believe that *karuna* is the instrument of moral order. While purity and perfection are easily comprehensible; Ambedkar's interpretation of them are commendable, as is his interpretation of "Dhamma is to give up craving"; but when Ambedkar says as having meant by the Buddha that "to live in *Nibbana* is *Dhamma*,[8] this view is certainly radical.

We may assimilate *Nibbana* and *karma* as down to earth postulates. What makes man unhappy is his falling a prey to his passions. These passions are called fetters which prevent man from reaching the state of *Nibbana*. Therefore, by *Nibbana* we can understand the conscious control of our passions, lust, infatuation and greed (*lobha*), hatred, anger, vexation or repugnance (*dosa*) and delusion, dullness and stupidity (*moha or avidya*).[9]

Connecting this with the belief that *karma* is the instrument of moral order, we may say that a person who has blown out his passions of *lobha, dosa* and *avidya* lives (here on earth) in *Nibbana* and therefore his *karma* constitutes a moral order while he yet lives or he attains *Parinibbana* (till he is totally extinguished by death). As a living person who attains *Nibbana* he gives up his craving and maintains purity of life; having realised that all compound things are impermanent, in addition to craving not for any impermanent, he has but to live a pure life; hence he reaches perfection in life. Thus, when one becomes a do-gooder, he is instrumental for a good moral order in society as believer that *karma* is the instrument of moral order. All these beliefs separately and together is *Dhamma*. Now the question is, is *Dhamma* a religion or a way of living or the way? This intricate difference is answered by Ambedkar in the succeeding chapters. There is one thing yet to be differenciated. That *karma* is interpreted as a synonym for morality. In what way this term comes into use, while *karma* in the traditional sense is used in terms of *karma* and rebirth? This too Ambedkar discusses later on.

In Book IV, Ambedkar first distinguishes between religion and *Dhamma*; then he explains how similarities in terminology conceal fundamental difference; then he expounds the Buddhist way of life and finally narrates the sermons of the Buddha. His attempts are to explain how Buddhism is an ideal religion—the best way of life.

In defining religion Ambedkar rightly says that the conception of religion was never fixed and that it has varied from time to time.[10] But in a sweeping statement he says "What the Buddha calls *Dhamma* is analogous to what the European theologians call Religion. Some European theologians refuse to recognise the *Buddha's Dhamma* as religion. There need be no regrets over this. The loss is theirs. It does no harm to the *Buddha's Dhamma*. Rather, it shows what is wanting in Religion...Religion is personal and one must keep it oneself... Contrary to this *Dhamma* is social. It is fundamentally and essentially so. *Dhamma* is righteousness which means right relations between man and man in all spheres of life. From this it is evident that one man if he is alone does not need *Dhamma*. But when there are two men living in relation to each other they must find a place for *Dhamma*, whether they like it or not. Neither can escape it".[11]

Discussing the meaning of the word *Dhamma*, Ambedkar advances his own explanatory additions. *Dhamma*, according to the Buddha, he says, consists of *prajna* and *karuna*, i.e., understanding and love which are the two corner-stones of *Dhamma*, leaving no room for superstition and this *Dhamma*. Further, he notably says: "Religion is concerned with revealing the beginning of things and *Dhamma* is not".[12] "The purpose of religion is to explain the origin of the world. The purpose of *Dhamma* is to reconstruct the world".[13] In the next sections he has placed morality as *Dhamma's* highest teaching. Ambedkar's approach is pragmatic and finds *Dhamma* far above the concept of religion and radically different.

Ambedkar grapples with the doctrine of karma. First he repudiates the common belief that the Buddhist doctrine of *karma* and that of the Brahminic doctrine of *karma* are one and the same. Ambedkar used some violent words like malicious propaganda. As the Brahminic (Hindu) understanding of the law of *karma* is, it allows the existence of a soul, which goes on from life to life. In Buddhism there is no soul, so the question does not arise. Though Ambedkar's explanation is good, his admonition that the Hindu version of *karma* is 'jugglery' reflects the temper of Ambedkar. To Ambedkar, Buddha's teaching of the law of *karma* is clean, when he said 'Reap as you sow', and refers to present life only.[14] It is not futuristic. Ambedkar says: "This is a very pernicious doctrine. For, in this interpretation of *karma*, there is no room left for human effort. Everything is pre-determined for him by his past karma"[15]. He concludes that "it is impossible to imagine that the Buddha who was known as the *Maha Karunika* could have supported such a doctrine"[16].

Thus the theories of *karma* and rebirth are reversed by Ambedkar as rebirth and *karma* as philosophical speculations and are two separate doctrinal issues. Unlike the traditional beliefs of one being related to the other, for Ambedkar's approach is limited to present life only.

On *Ahimsa* Ambedkar says: "there is no subject which is a matter of greater confusion than this subject of *Ahimsa*".[17] He cites examples that the monks of Ceylon fought against the foreign invaders and that they asked the people of Ceylon to fight; on the other hand the monks of Burma did the opposite when foreigners invaded Burma; the German Buddhist Association passed a resolution that they will accept all Panch Silas except the first, i.e., on *Ahimsa*.[18] As the Buddha has not given any definition of *Ahimsa*, Ambedkar gives his understanding of the Buddha's attitude towards *Ahimsa* by 'circumstantial evidence' (Ambedkar was a Bar-at-law).

The evidence that Ambedkar finds is that the Buddha did not have any objection to eating meat if offered as alms. He resisted the oppression of Devadatta who insisted that the monks should be prohibited from eating meat given to them by way of alms... he was only opposed to killing of animals in *yagna* (sacrifice).[19] Ambedkar asserts that *Ahimsa Puranao Dharma* is an extreme doctrine that of Jains and not the Buddha[20]. Ambedkar quotes the Buddha "Love all so that you may not wish to kill anyone" and therefore "it is quite clear that the Buddha meant to make a distinction between will to kill and need to kill. He did not ban killing where there was need to kill"[21]. Here again Ambedkar shows the middle path of the Buddha: "Brahminism has in it the will to kill, Jainism has in it the will never to kill; The Buddha's *Ahimsa* is quite in keeping with his middle path ... He did not make *Ahimsa* a matter of rule. He enunciated it as a matter of principle or way of life"[22].

Book V of the *Buddha and His Dhamma* is devoted to the *Sangha*, i.e., the monastic order. Here Ambedkar discusses at length the *Sangha*, the Bhikku —and the Duties of the Bhikku. Part I deals with *Sangha and its organisation*.

Part II of Book V deals with the Buddha's conception of what a Bhikku should be. Also he differenciates the Bhikku from an ascetic. The Bhikku and the Brahmin, Bhikku and the Upasaka. The Buddha set some ideals for a Bhikku, in addition to his external appearance, but also rigid inner demands and virtues, interior and exterior. Ambedkar quotes 23 ideals which he would expect of a Bhikku. There are eight more ideals, which Ambedkar writes not as quotation, but referring as "the Disciples of Gautama (Buddha)".

Part III of Book V deals with the duties of the Bhikku. Here, the Bhikku's main duty is to convert, but that conversion is not to be effected by miracles, nor by force. A Bhikku must spread virtue.

Part IV of Book V provides a comparative analysis of the Bhikku and Upasaka. The *Parivrajaka* is not accepted into the *Sangha* as a member unless and untill he is initiated after *upasampada* by a ceremony called *Sangha-Diksha*. In a bold statement Ambedkar says that "the *Sangha* was an independent body. It was independent even of its founder"[23]. The Bhikku had his living by alms and the laity took care of the Bhikkus by giving alms. "*Sangha Diksha* included both initiation into the *Sangha* as well as with *Dhamma*. One important observation that Ambedkar makes is that" ...there was no separate *Dhamma Diksha* for those who wanted to be initiated into the *Dhamma*, but did not wish to become members of the *Sangha*" (i.e., who did not want to become Bhikkus)... "This was a grave omission. It was one of the causes which ultimately led to the downfall of Buddhism in India. For, this absence of the initiation ceremony left the laity to wander from one religion to another and, worse still, follow at one and the same time"[24]. Ambedkar observes that the bond of alms was good enough to reform an erring laity as well correct an erring monk. For Ambedkar, "*Vinaya Pitaka* is nothing but redress of complaints of the laity"[25]. In the next chapter Ambedkar explains that *Dhamma* as preached by the Buddha is the same for both Bhikkus and laity. Only their code of conduct and possessions differed. "A Bhikku is free to enter *Parinibbana*; *Nibbana* is enough for layman ... *Dhamma*, however, is the same for both"[26].

In Part V, i.e., *Vinaya* for laity, Ambedkar lays down different disciplines for the wealthy, the householder, children, pupil, husband and wife, master and servant, girls and cites one householder's decision to become lay-disciple of the Buddha. The Buddha insisted that the acquisition of riches must be subject to *Vinaya*"[27]. Thus Ambedkar presents Buddhism to the laity as world-affirming; *Vinaya* for the householder as respect and reverence for his parents, teachers, wife and children, friends and companions, his servants and workmen (last in the hierarchy) his religious teachers; *Vinaya* for children is that they must minister to their parents; the same *Vinaya* is for the pupil too. For husband and wife, mutual respect and care; for master and servant, care for the servant on the part of the master and ministering with love to the master on the part of the servant. Ambedkar also includes in this chapter that clansman should minister to religious teachers by action and the religious teachers should restrain them from evil and exhort them to do good, correct and purify what has heard and teach what has not been heard. Finally, in the last chapter, the Buddha gives a fairly long piece of counselling to the girls (spinsters), who would be future brides: They are to be faithful to the chores of housewife, getting up early, last to retire, do all domestics, respect husband's people, develop husband's home-crafts, care and tend the sick, and taking care of the silver and gold of the husband.

Book VI is on Buddha and his contemporaries, friends and foes, critics and admirers. Book VII records the events prior to the Buddha's demise and ends with his death. Book VIII is all about the Buddha, all in praise of the Buddha. An eulogy on every aspect of the Buddha. Though this may not constitute the doctrine, but it would be the text for Neo-Buddhists, to draw inspiration from the Buddha's life.

The foregone pages being the quint essence of the message in *Buddha and His Dhamma*, objective reader has to acknowledge Dr. Ambedkar's profound understanding of the Buddhist doctrines. This apart, it is obvious that he had also read the Hindu literature and the *Bible* thoroughly well.

In the entire *opus*, the influence of the *Bible* is evident both in style and form. There are five Books; he had not named them like in the *Bible*, but gives Roman numerals instead; each Book, like in the *Bible* has chapters and verses. The language is often typical of King James version of the *Bible*, interspersed with contemporary English.

The first episode that a reader wonders finding is that Ambedkar for whom supernatural element is not the rationale, writes of the birth of Gautama which is very much similar to the annunciation of Virgin Mary in the *Bible*."...They bathed her, robed her in a dress anointed her with perfumes and decked her with flowers in a manner fit to meet some divinity. Then a Bodhisattva, by name Sumedha appeared before her saying "I have decided to take my last and final birth on this earth, will you consent to be my mother?" She said, "yes with great pleasure". At this moment Mahamaya woke. Next morning Mahamaya told her dream to Suddhodana. Not knowing how to interpret the dream, Suddhodana summoned eight Brahmins who were most famous in divination... The Brahmin said, "Be not anxious (cf: Fear not Mary, you shall bear a son...). You will have a son and if he leads a householder's life, he will become universal monarch and if he leaves his home and goes forth into a homeless state and becomes a Sanyasi, he will become a Buddha, a dispeller of illusions in the world..."[28]* These involve the phenomenon of dream, interpretation of dream with a prophetic connotation—typical of Biblical style. Only the style of pronouns is

* This passage is free adoptation of the (Annunciation of virgin Mary in the *Bible*). And the Angel Gabril said unto Mary...Fear not Mary...you shall bear a son... He shall be great and shall be called son of the Highest and he shall reign for ever and ever...Cf. St. Luke 1:26-35.

unsteady—at times 'you' at times 'Thou', etc., and modern phrases are often used.

Finally, the doctrinal difference between traditional Buddhism and Neo-Buddhism, as seen earlier, is conspicuous one: the elimination of the four Noble Truths. This apart, as noted, Ambedkar had prescribed 22 vows and had retained the Noble eight-fold path. The five precepts and the ten *parimittas* are also important doctrinal beliefs of a Neo-Buddhist.

1. Noble Eight-fold Path:

1. Right belief
2. Right thought and right aims
3. Right speech
4. Right conduct
5. Right means of livelihood
6. Right effort
7. Right mindfulness
8. Right meditation

2. Five Precepts:

1. I shall abstain from harming living beings.
2. I shall abstain from taking not given.
3. I shall abstain from sexual misconduct.
4. I shall abstain from false speech.
5. I shall abstain from indulging in intoxicating drinks and drugs.

3. The Parimittas:

1. *Sila* (moral temperament)
2. *Dana* (the giving, charity)
3. *Uppekka* (detachment)

4. *Nekkema* (renunciation of the pleasures of the world)
5. *Virya* (right endeavour)
6. *Kanthi* (forbearance)
7. *Succa* (truth)
8. *Adhishana* (right determination)
9. *Karuna* (loving kindness)
10. *Maitri* (Extending fellow feeling to all—friend or foe).

4. The Three Refuges:

The *Trisarana* or *Three Refuges* bind Neo-Buddhists with the Buddhist fraternity all over the world. They are:

1. Refuge in the Buddha
2. Refuge in the *Dhamma*
3. Refuge in the *Sangha*

The Third Refuge, viz., taking 'Refuge in the *Sangha*' is, at present, a meaningless phrase for a Neo-Buddhist. However, a Neo-Buddhist takes this 'Refuge', both to be in conformity with the tradition in the Buddhist world and in the fervent hope that the Neo-Buddhist Sangha may become a reality.

5. The Twenty-two Vows[29]:

The *twenty-two vows*, prescribed by Dr. Ambedkar for Neo-Buddhist converts, give a separate identity for Neo-Buddhists, within the World Federation of Buddhists. This is unique in the sense that it was prescribed in the Indian context.

1. I shall not recognise Brahma, Vishnu and Mahesh as gods, nor shall I worship them.
2. I shall not recognise Rama and Krishna as gods, nor shall I worship them.
3. I shall not recognise Gowri and Ganpati as gods nor shall I worship them.

4. I do not believe in the theory of incarnation of God.
5. I do not consider the Buddha as the incarnation of Vishnu.
6. I shall not perform shradh for my ancestors, nor shall I give offerings to God.
7. I shall not do anything which is detrimental to Buddhism.
8. I shall not perform any religious rite through the agency of a Brahman.
9. I believe in the principle that all human beings are equal.
10. I shall endeavour to establish equality.
11. I shall follow the Eight-fold path of the Buddha.
12. I shall observe the ten *Parimittas* enunciated by the Buddha.
13. I shall be compassionate to all living beings and I shall nurture them with care.
14. I shall not steal.
15. I shall not lie.
16. I shall not commit adultery.
17. I shall not take liquor.
18. I shall not strive to lead my life according to the three principles of Buddhism, i.e., *Gyan, Sheel* and *Karuna.*
19. I hereby reject my old religion Hinduism which is detrimental to the prosperity of human kind which discriminates between man and man and accept Buddhism.
20. I fully believe that Buddhism is Saddhamma.
21. I believe that I am reborn now.

22. I pledge to conduct myself hereafter in accordance with Buddha's Dhamma.

The twenty-two vows which Dr. Ambedkar prescribed for all the Neo-Buddhists look superfluous to on-looker. But when we connect these vows to the context of mass conversion we would be convinced that it was necessary that these become part of the Neo-Buddhist Doctrines, in addition to the already existing Buddhist Doctrines.

To counter the evils of the then existing Hindu Society, Ambedkar evolved twenty-two vows, and made people realise that living in Buddhism, is being 'dead' to Hinduism. These vows constitute more of a sociological pedagogy than denouncing Hindu theology and avowing to enter the portals of Buddhist ideology. The sequence in which the vows are arranged is in fact disarrayed. It is not known whether Ambedkar deliberately kept these in this pattern, or if they were in the order of his spontaneous thoughts. Let us consider them in the following sequence:

The *first five vows* are negation of Hindu deities. Ambedkar, by making his followers deny these five precepts, makes all the people realise that Buddhism has nothing to do with Hindu beliefs. The *eighth vow* is to show that the office of priesthood to perform rites of any kind is no more needed. Hence first five and the eighth vow marks the total severence of the Mahars from Hinduism. This could be best effected only by making them take on oath or vow to this effect and that Ambedkar got accomplished.

The *sixth vow* is regarding the concept and meaning of death. In the traditional Hindu belief the soul of a person leaves that body to be born again. But for a Buddhist it is *Parinibbana,* i.e., total extinguishing or blowing out. There is no soul and therefore there is no rebirth of that soul. Now in the *twenty-first vow,* a Neo-Buddhist is reborn—a new life in Buddhism.

The *9th* and *10th vows* are in line with the principle of equality the out-castes have been fighting for since the time Dr. Ambedkar returned from his higher studies abroad. They wanted equality of social status, which was possible in Buddhism. Having accepted Buddhism, they have attained it. In Buddhism as we know all are equal and so are the Neo-Buddhists. Having attained it, now it was the new responsibility of all Neo-Buddhists to endeavour to establish equality.

13th to *17th vows* are relating to the social ethics that is badly needed in any society. Therefore, he had included the clauses of being compassionate, not to steal, not to utter lies, and not to take liquor.

18th vow is striving to lead a life according to the three principles of Buddhism—*prajna, sila* and *karuna*. Here Ambedkar is introducing the lofty ideals of Buddhism.

The *19th vow* ought is a solemn oath of rejection of Hinduism and acceptance of Buddhism.

The remaining vows could have been in this order:

20th vow, 11th vow, 12th vow, 22nd vow and 7th vow.

These vows are very important as the Mahar converts of that time were an ignorant mass. These words must have instilled great joy to understand what they were doing as they were taking the vow.

On the whole, Ambedkar with his astute wisdom included these vows along with the other ceremonial vows to be taken by a convert at the time of Diksha. These vows mark a separate identity for the Neo-Buddhists, simple and straight. There is no need to read the voluminous canonical literature that is there in Buddhism.

There are complicated doctrines in Buddhism, namely, Hinayana, Mahayana, 2Vajrayana, Tantrayana. But Navayana or Bhimayana or Neo-Buddhism, is a simple and a straight faith.

REFERENCES

1. Kadam, K.N. (ed.), *op.cit.*, p. 57.
2. *Ibid.*, p. 57.
3. Sangharakshita, *op. cit.*, pp. 147-48.
4. Ambedkar, Dr. B.R., *Buddha and His Dhamma*, Introduction.
5. Sangharakshita *op. cit.*, p. 152.
6. *Ibid.*, p. 153.
7. Ambedkar Dr. B.R., *op. cit.*, II P. III-1-1 to 21.
8. *Ibid.*, B II/Part III-5-vs 1 ff.
9. *Ibid.*, B III/Part III-3-35-37.
10. *Ibid.*, IV/Part I-1-vs. 4, 5.
11. *Ibid.*, IV/Part I-2-vs. 1 to 11.
12. *Ibid.*, IV/Part -2-1-31.
13. *Ibid.*, IV/Part I-3-15.
14. *Ibid.*, p. 338, vs. 1, 3.
15. *Ibid.*, p. 339, vs. 7.
16. *Ibid.*, p. 344, vs. 23.
17. *Ibid.*, p. 345, vs. 5.
18. *Ibid.*, p. 345, vs. 8 to 12.
19. *Ibid.*, p. 346, vs. 4 to 7.
20. *Ibid.*, p. 346, vs. 8.
21. *Ibid.*, p. 346, vs. 9, 12.
22. *Ibid.*, p. 347, vs. 18 to 22.
23. *Ibid.*, p. 451, vs. 4.
24. *Ibid.*, p. 451, vs. 11 to 13.
25. *Ibid.*, p. 452, vs. 5.
26. *Ibid.*, p. 459, vs. 47, 49.
27. *Ibid.*, p. 459, vs. 3.
28. Ambedkar, *op. cit.*, (Book I, Ch. 3, vs. 9-11, 16).
29. *Ambedkar Lehar*, London, 1978, p. 3.

6

THE ETHICO-RITUALISTIC DIMENSION OF NEO-BUDDHISM

In *Buddha and His Dhamma,* Dr. Ambedkar posits a well-defined code of ethical conduct which needs to be studied as a dimension by itself. The rituals associated with Traditional Buddhism are reduced to mere ceremonies by him. This chapter is to project this dimension.

ETHICS

Ethics is the science of morals. In Neo-Buddhism we see that Ethics and *Dhamma* are presented as synonymous. Morality and *Dhamma* are so intermixed that Neo-Buddhist doctrines and Neo-Buddhist Ethics are inseparable even for analytic study. There is a heavy overlapping. Ambedkar has said, "Morality is *Dhamma* and *Dhamma* is morality. In other words, in *Dhamma* morality takes the place of God, although there is no God in *Dhamma*.... It is not to please God that man has to be moral. It is for his own good that man has to love man."[1] Since Ambedkar's interpretation of Buddhism is layman-oriented, ethics has a vital role in its spiritual-doctrinal management.

As far as the Bhikkus are concerned there is absolute rigidity on their total conduct. But for layman it is mostly an obligation. Buddhism has placed the *Dhamma* as common and same for both the monk and laity, the difference being that while for the Bhikkus total compliance to the rules is a *Must*, for Laity it is a mere *may*, though by rule it should be a *Must*. The five precepts and the eight-fold path in addition to the first and foremost *Tri-sharana* are same for every Buddhist.

1. Neo-Buddhist Ethics

The most authentic version of Neo-Buddhist Ethics is to be seen in Part III of Book IV in *Buddha and His Dhamma*. Here Ambedkar compiles all ethical codes of conduct in the entire canonical literature, edits them, adds his own comments and has listed them. The first such 'Buddhist Way of Life'is Do good. Be party to no evil. Commit no sin. This is the Buddhist way of life "....Happy is the heaping of good.... Treat not lightly of evil... follow not after things evil... cherish not false ideas. Hasten towards the excellent, suppress all evil thoughts.... If a man commits sin, let him not do it again, let him not delight in sin, the accumulation of evil is painful..."[2]. Ambedkar goes on preaching as a teacher of proverbs or *Nitisloka*.

The second chapter is on craving and lust, "Do not be possessed by craving or lust. This is the Buddhist way of life" ..."from craving is born sorrow, from craving is born fear. To him who is wholly free from craving there is neither sorrow nor fear" (well, if Ambedkar has rejected the *Arya Satyas*, he seems to bring it in as a moral code!).

Ambedkar lists grief as an offshoot of pleasure, attachment, lust and greed.

The third chapter begins with, "cause no hurt, cherish no ill-will. This is the Buddhist way of life.... To speak no ill, to do no harm, to practice restraint in conformity with discipline. This is the counsel of the Buddha". Then Ambedkar writes: "Kill (not) nor cause slaughter". This is an important ethical code, for while dealing with *Ahimsa* as doctrine he had positively written that a layman may kill (according to the situation, probably he had country's defence in mind). Here in ethics "killing or causing slaughter is forbidden ...". He who seeking his own happiness does not punish or kill beings who also long for happiness, *will* find happiness.... If a man offends a harmless, pure and innocent person, the evil falls back upon that fool, like light dust thrown up against the wind"[3].

The fourth chapter begins with: "cherish no anger. Forget your enmities, win your enemies by love. This is the Buddhist way of life.... Let a man overcome anger by love, let him overcome evil by good;* let him overcome the greedy by liberality, the liar by truth... There is no fire like lust, no ill fortune like hatred. There is no misery like the constituents of existence, no happiness higher than the peace of *Nibbana.* For hatred does not cease by hatred at any time; hatred ceases by love...."[4]

The fifth chapter is on Man, Mind and Impurities. "Man is what his mind makes him. This is somewhat similar to the Latin proverb: *Mens agitat Molem* (Mind moves the matter). The training of the mind to seek the good, is the first step in the path of Righteousness. This is the main teaching in the Buddhist way of life....Hard to control,

* Here Ambedkar's knowledge of Christian ethics is evident. Cf. St. Mathew 5:43 'Love your enemies' (Jesus Christ): Romans 12:21 'Do not be overcome by evil, but overcome evil with good' (St. Paul). Ambedkar has obviously been influenced deeply by Christian teachings, but communicates Buddhist ideals in his own language—Author.

unstable is this mind, ever in quest of delight. Good is it to subdue the mind. A mind subdued brings happiness. ...Let a wise man blow off the impurities of himself, as a smith blows off the impurities of silver one-by-one, little-by-little, and from time-to-time...But there is a taint worse than all taints, Ignorance is the greatest taint. Oh! mendicants, throw off that taint and become taintless. ...And the man who gives himself to drinking intoxicating liquors, he even in this world, digs up his own grave.... There is no fire like passion, there is no torrent like greed.... Refrain from all evil; cultivate the good; cleanse your own thoughts; this is the teaching of the Buddha".[5] Very stimulating indeed.

The sixth chapter is on self and self-conquest. "If one has self, let him practice self-conquest. This is the Buddhist way of life... self is the lord of self, who else could be the Lord? With self well subdued, a man finds a Lord as few can find.... He who loves looking for pleasures only, his senses uncontrolled, immoderate in his food, idle and weak, will certainly be overthrown by his own overdoing as the wind throws down a weak tree.... First establish Thyself in the right, then thou mayest counsel others. Let not the wiseman give occasion for reproach".[6] (Note the change of the pronoun to olden days' English). This is the quintessence of this chapter.

The seventh chapter is on the ethics of wisdom, justice and good company. It reads as "Be wise, be just and choose good company. This is the Buddhist way of life.... Wise people after they have listened to the Dhamma become serene, like a deep, smooth and still lake.... If a fool be associated with a wiseman even all his life, he will perceive the truth as little as a spoon perceives the taste of soup.... A man is not just if he carries a matter by violence; no, he who distinguishes both right and wrong, who is learned and guides others, not by violence, but by the same *Dhamma*, being a guardian of the Dhamma and intelligent, he is called just... It is better to live alone, there is no companionship with a fool; let a man walk alone, commit no sin, with few wishes, like an elephant in the forest.... He who walks in the company of fools suffers a long way: Company with fools as with an enemy, is always painful; company with the wise is pleasure, like meeting with kinsfolk. Therefore, one ought to follow the wise, the intelligent, the learned, the much enduring, the dutiful, the elect, one ought to follow such a good and wiseman, as the moon follows the path of the stars...."[7]

The eighth chapter is on thoughtfulness and mindfulness: "In everything be thoughtful. In everything be mindful; In all things be earnest and bold. This is the Buddhist way of life. All that we are is the result of what we have thought. It is founded on our thoughts; it is made up of our thoughts. If a man speaks or acts with an evil thought, pain follows him.... Be not thoughtless, watch your thoughts. Draw yourself out of the evil way like an elephant sunk in mud. Let the wise man guard his thoughts.... thoughts well guarded bring happiness.... This mind of mine (Ambedkar's? hopefully not) went formerly wandering about as it liked, as it listed, as it pleased; but I shall now hold it in thoroughly, as the elder who holds the hook holds the furious elephant.... Not a mother, not a father will do so much nor any other relatives as a well directed mind will do us...."[8]

The ninth chapter is on vigilance, earnestness and boldness. This chapter does not begin with the usual couplets ending with ..."this is the Buddhist way of life". (So let us assume "Be vigilant, be earnest and be bold; this is the Buddhist way of life!) "Vigilant among the negligent, awake among those asleep'..... so go to the wise.... Earnestless leads to where death is not; heedlessness is the way of death. Those who continue in earnestness do not die, but the heeders are as if already dead. Fall not away from your purpose for the sake of another, however great this latter may be. When once you have seen your goal, hold it firm and fast...."[9]

The tenth chapter is on sorrow and happiness; on charity and kindness: "Poverty gives rise to sorrow, but removal of poverty, does not necessarily give rise to happiness. Not a high standard of living, but a high standard of culture is what gives happiness. This is the Buddhist way of life. Hunger is the worst of diseases. Health is the greatest of gifts, contentedness, the best of riches; trust is the best of relationships; *Nibbana*, the highest happiness.... Charity to *Dhamma* exceeds all gifts. Liberty, courtesy, goodwill and unselfishness, these are to the world what the lynch pin to the chariot. This is the Buddhist way of life".[10]

The eleventh chapter is on hypocrisy: ".... As the perfect one speaks, so he acts; as the perfect one acts, so he speaks. And because he speaks as he acts and acts as he speaks, therefore he is called the perfect one. This is the Buddhist way of life..."[11]

The twelfth chapter is on following the right way: "Choose the Right Way. Depart not from it. There are many paths: not all lead to the Right Way.... The best way is the eight-fold way: the best truths, the four words: the best of virtues passionlessness... (Let us note that "the best truths, the four words—or four truths? —the four noble truths? —What did Ambedkar mean? If this refers to four noble truths, how did Ambedkar let this in?) .... Do not follow the evil law! Do not live on thoughtlessness! Do not follow false doctrine! Rouse yourself! Do not be idle! follow the law of virtue! The virtuous rests in bliss in this world.... Beware of the anger of the tongue and control your tongue. Leave the sins of the mind, and practice virtue with thy mind. Earnestness is the path of *Nirvana*, thoughtlessness is the path of death"[12].

The last chapter is thirteenth, compiled by Ambedkar entitled "Mix not true *Dhamma* with false *Dhamma*". "Those who mistake false for true and true for false, there abides wrong-mindedness—they arrive not at the truth... Those who know true as ture and false as false, there abides right mindedness—these arrive at the truth"[13].

In the foregoing pages excerpts highlighting the ethical teachings of Buddhism were presented. As we browse through them, they appear to be wisdom literature selected from various sources, of course, within the Buddhist sources. While some of them are in line with Ambedkar's pragmatic approach, others appear to be hypothetical. In the absence of exact source references, it is difficult to accept all that was said was that of Buddha and for Ambedkar, this was very important. The ethical teachings submitted may be taken as the moral teachings for Neo-Buddhists and their literature for profitable reading. The ethical teachings have doctrinal undertones.

2. Sermons on Conduct

In addition to the Buddhist way of life, Ambedkar had included some of the sermons of the Buddha, some of which are pertaining to Ethics, ethics of relationship or code of conduct.

The most impressive of these sermons compiled by Ambedkar is the one that the Buddha gave, when the king got upset on receiving the news that his queen gave birth to a girl. The Buddha in those days, when women were considered in a poor esteem, boldly told the king that a female child may prove even a better off spring than male and gives reasons why. The Buddha concludes his sermon saying that the son of a noble wife becomes country's guide. In the eyes of the Buddha, women were never seen as inferior to men, that too two and half milleniums ago!

There is a sermon of the Buddha on the relationship between husband and wife and their living together. Some are well matched, some ill-matched. An ideal man and an ideal woman, a wicked man and an ideal woman, an ideal man and a wicked woman, and a wicked man and a wicked woman. The first cited couple are like god and goddess. The rest are vile.

The Buddha laid great emphasis on one's character and so did Ambedkar. In a sermon, the Buddha narrates how a man could have his downfall. Eleven reasons are furnished by the Buddha. They are: (i) Hating *Dhamma* (Intellectual); (2) Bad Company; (3) Laziness; (4) Irresponsibility towards one's parents; (5) Cheating a Brahmin or ascetic or monk; (6) Miserliness; (7) Arrogance; (8) Squandering; (9) Adultery; (10) Misplaced trust; and (11) Unreasonably ambitious. This is all inclusive ethical code of conduct.

In another sermon, while explaining who a wicked man is (one who finds faults with others without being asked, talks ill of others openly is a wicked man), says the Buddha, we ought not to talk ill of others; we have to be open and frank. Similarly, giving a sermon on the best man, the Buddha says that the best man is one who strives for the welfare of not only others, but himself as well; the traditional suggestion that one must not be selfish, but care more for others first—such a man is rated by the Buddha as good, but not good enough. Do good to others but you should do the same to yourself as well. Such a person is topmost, highest and supreme.

In the fourth sermon that Ambedkar had compiled, the Buddha answering an enquirer says that he is neither a *Deva* nor a *Ghandharva,* nor a *Yaksa* nor even a man. To the perplexed enquirer who wants to know who the Buddha then is, the latter replies that he was an enlightened one. In this context, the Buddha implies that an enlightened person is one who does not a consume intoxicants. The Buddha says that he was once could be deemed a *Deva* or a *Ghandharva* or a *Yaksha* or for that matter a man as long as he used to take intoxicants. Now that he had cut out from the root consuming intoxicants, he could be considered an enlightened one. In other words, a Buddhist cannot consume liquor.

In the fifth sermon, the Buddha classifies men into four kinds: first those who do all acts of self-mortification themselves, but do urge the same on others; second, those who neither do themselves nor urge others to do the same; third, those who urge others to extirpate their evil habits, but not on themselves; and the fourth, those who extirpate all their evils and urge others to do. The fourth category of persons would be deemed to be just and good.

In the sixth sermon, the Buddha urges people to do good works. The Buddha suggests three good acts, namely, deeds of charity, self-taming (of tongue) and self-control.

In the seventh sermon, the Buddha says that there is a "great need for good resolutions to be made and observed for a pure and happy life.... Resolve that `all my life-long may I support my parents. May I respect the head of my clan. May I be of gentle speech. May I speak evil of none, clearing my heart of the stain of selfishness, may I dwell at home generous, pure handed, delighting in giving up. May I be a proper man to ask a boon of, delighting in sharing gifts with others. All my life-long may I be angerless, and if anger arises, may I quickly check it"[14]. In other words, the Buddha exhorts his followers to become perfect as human beings.

3. Sermons on Righteousness

As in the *Dhamma,* Righteousness is of paramount importance, Ambedkar had compiled a series of sermons of the Buddha exclusively on all the aspects of Righteousness. In the first of the sermons compiled on Righteousness, the Buddha sets forth what Righteousness is, by defining first what unrighteousness is. The Buddha says that there are "three forms of unrighteousness and wickedness for the body; four for speech; and three for thoughts"[15]. The three bodily unrighteousness would be that a man may take life, may take what is not his, may be a fornicator. Regarding unrighteousness of speech a man may be a liar, may be a slanderer, may be hurtful and wounding others and may be a tattler. Regarding unrighteousness of thought, a man may be covetous or may be malevolent and wicked of heart, or may be wrong in outlook and erroneous in his conceptions.

On the contrary, the Buddha says that there are three forms of righteousness and goodness for the body, four for speech and three for thoughts. As regards bodily righteousness, first, "a man puts from him all killing and abstains from killing anything; laying aside cudgel and sword, he lives a life of innocence and mercy, full of kindness and compassion for everything that lives"[16]. (Here *Ahimsa* is preached in its fullest sense; here the position of the Buddha is firm in total *Ahimsa,* urging one to put off sword and cudgel unlike the position of Ambedkar.) Second, he would not commit any theft, takes only what is his, thus lives an honest life; third, there is no sensual misconduct and one abstains from fornication. Regarding Righteousness of speech, he would not utter lies and is not a slanderer, and abstains from bitter speech. Regarding righteousness of thoughts, a man is to be devoid of conveteousness, harbours no malevalence, and is right in outlook and correct in his conceptions.

In the second sermon the need of righteousness is emphasised. The immoral man, i.e., the unrighteous suffers losses. The righteous man, on the other hand, becomes wealthy by his own exertions; he is honoured everywhere; he enters any place with boldness and confidence; and he enjoys peace of mind and he passes away with an untroubled mind. The fool does not know his folly. His own deeds will, like a fire, consume him. Anyone who offends the innocent will suffer great disaster, or disturbed mind, looses his relations and loses all his wealth. This sermon is addressed to the laity.

The third sermon is on a householder, who is a cunning fleecer and is corrected by a monk. This is consequent to an enquiry which was assigned by the Buddha to that monk. This householder had lost his earlier zeal, earnestness and righteousness as he had to support his parents, his wife, family and servants and in addition do his obligations to the deities and the king. This householder is corrected by the monk that no matter what happens one has to walk in righteousness and equity.

The fourth sermon of the Buddha is on how to reach perfection in righteous conduct. This, again, is addressed to the laity. The principles that the Buddha suggests are these: no killing, no thieving, no incontinence, no lying, no drinking (liquor), no luxury or perfume; to make vows regularly, to offer vows every morning and after that with thankful and pious heart, to be wise and to give alms; to cherish parents well, and to follow a righteous (honest?) trade.

Last of the sermons of the Buddha compiled on righteousness by Ambedkar is that "one need not wait for a companion to tread on the path of righteousness". These teachings on tongues are indeed very moving. (As) an elephant in battle bears the arrow at him hurled, I must bear men's bitter tongues for every evil in the world. Tamed, they lead him into battle; tamed the king on his back ascends; (like this bitter tongue) tamed he is the best of beings when no bitter speech affords. Good are well-tamed mules, and good are Indian steeds of lineage famed, good indeed are the mighty tusker; best of all men is self-tamed. (All great writers have written about the evil of tongues. Thiruvalluvar, the great Tamil poet, had written: the wounds of arrows will heal, not the wounds of the tongue. It is not out of place to mention that it is said that he was of lowly birth and a Buddhist.) Buddha used this allegory and continues, "yet such mounts can, naught avail us, cannot be Nibbana's guide. We can only reach the path on self-tamed, self-ride"[17]. In one illustration the Buddha delivers three messages: *First,* we must bear the hurt of biting and bitter tongues (abuses) hurled at us. *Second,* like the wild animals are tamed for our use, so also the tongue must be tamed. *Third,* however well wild animals may be tamed and trained, they cannot help us to walk on the path of lasting values—like *Nibbana*—of life. So also, we need not wait for someone to help us to walk in the path of righteousness. This is not in agreement with the Judaistic-Christian belief that "He (The Lord) shall lead me in the paths of righteousness" (Psalm 23:3). In the absence of God, morality takes His place and righteousness is synonymous with morality. The Buddha, in continuation, exhorts his listeners to expunge all evil thoughts.

Ambedkar has assimilated all these teachings of the Buddha to be presented in modern language. As noted, he had doubted whether all the quotations of the Buddha as found in the canonical literature were the Buddha's own words or later accretions by the monks. Similarly, the language used in the explanation for "Expunging all bad thoughts", by the style, vocabulary and vehemence, makes one wonder whether these ethical codes were those of the Buddha himself or later accretions by Dr. Ambedkar! The doubt is caused by using intricate words subtly translated, specially the last with forceful vehemence. This passage appears unlike the Buddha's calm sobriety.

4. An Estimate

'The *Buddha and His Dhamma* is the only Neo-Buddhist material, which serves as 'scriptural' text as well as code of conduct, to augment the needs for Doctrines and Ethics for the Neo-Buddhists. What Ambedkar has done deserves to be lauded as he had brought forth a concise Neo-Buddhist 'Bible' to cater to the needs of the mass converts. This has since been translated into Hindi and almost every Neo-Buddhist has this at home. The emphasis on social equality, casteless society and importance of the laity in Buddhism appeals to the Neo-Buddhist mass of today. Equally appealing is the consistency of the message, use of Pali words to denote 'who' or 'what' (like Parivrajaka, Bhikku) instead of English words, very specially in the last Book and chapters on the Buddha himself. There could be possibilities that a scholar could find fault with the book as it lacks references to sources. Here two things have to be borne in mind: First, no scripture bears sources of reference; Secondly, Ambedkar finished the opus more or less in a hurry and unfortunately did not live even to see the printed book. What a dispassionate student needs to do is to take the best of the message and the author to assess if the work has done its objective, which *Buddha and His Dhamma* has amply done.

Probably, the greatest contribution of Ambedkar rendered to Buddhism in India is providing the Neo-Buddhists with a 'concise' canon, however, controversial it may be. *Buddha and His Dhamma* is a simple Doctrinal and Ethical guide post with single strand of thought unlike the manifold and confusing Yanas. If only the Aryan truths were included in it, it would have posed no problem for Buddhists of either sects—Hinayana and Mahayana. Its absence is very conspicuous and we may repeat Ambedkar's very phrase on him—They are 'stumbling block' for any Buddhist (and non-Buddhist), Neo-Buddhists apart. The most important feature of any canonical text of a religion is its central teaching and Ambedkar has done well to maintain the centrality of *Theravada* (minus Aryan truths), high-lighting morality as the *summun bonum* and very strictly enforcing and stressing the importance of total abstinence from intoxicants.

When Dr. Ambedkar brought out *The Constitution of India*, he was then hailed as the modern Manu. We may, in our context, say that *Buddha and His Dhamma* is the Veda of the Neo-Buddhists and Dr. Ambedkar be deemed as their Vyas!

We may conclude by saying that Dr. Babasaheb Ambedkar adopted teachings of the Buddha and developed it into Neo-Buddhism like Adi Sankara adopted the philosophy of Gaudapada and developed into non-Dualism, it may be added that while Sankara's interpretation made Gaudapada's philosophy loftier, Ambedkar's interpretation made Buddha's teachings simpler.

RITUALS

Commenting on the sermon preached first by the Buddha at Saranath to his first five disciples, Ambedkar notes in his *Buddha and His Dhamma* that the Buddha's path which is his Dhamma has no concern with rituals and ceremonies.[18] One of the major aspects of Buddhism is that it revolted against the established practice of sacrifices. The frequent ceremonies or rites of passage of the Hindu orthodoxy was rejected by the Buddha, for his path was living a simple and practical life arrived at *Nibbana*. Thus there was no christening ceremony, mundan ceremony*, sacred-thread ceremony**.... even at death, no such related ceremonies. The Buddhist society was one bereft of 'God' as the nucleus. Moral conduct, treading in the path of righteousness where reverence for elders, mutual love and respect between spouses and between man and man, concern and service between master and servant, physical care and spiritual admonition between the laity and the Bhikku, must have differentiated the gay, mirth and ritualistic Hindu society from the sober Buddhist community and from a self-mortifying Jain community. Therefore, the word "Ritual" seems to be out of place in the Buddhist context. Strictly speaking what we can safely say is that what could have been a 'Ritual' became certain ceremonies in course of time to administer certain functions.

The Buddha's approach was to converse and convince. Some became wholly devoted monks (Parivrajakas)—

* First shaving of hair on a child's herd.

** Wearing of long threads across the body ceremoneously.

giving up everything to the cause of the *Dhamma,* while a vast majority remained as householders (*upasakas*), who would accept the *Dhamma* as their way of life, while retaining and maintaining their vocations and professions. The monks *(Bhikkus)* were going about taking alms with the message of the *Dhamma.* Along with *Bhikkus, Bhikkunis*—women who had adopted the *Dhamma* and had given up the worldly affairs—there was no initiation for the laity which, according to Ambedkar, was a great omission. May be, that the Buddha did not have any such binding, even if there was when they accepted the *Dhamma's* five precepts and the eight-fold path. While the monks had a binding of vows and lived amongst their own communities, there was no such community-life for the Buddhist laity.

The Neo-Buddhist community has a different situation. For them the *Dhamma* is projected as Dhamma for the laity as an important factor and purpose of living, the style of living itself had changed from the very minute of mass conversion. They had become a separate identity, where they need not wait upon a *purohit* (clergy) to conduct any *Samskara* (Ritual). Ambedkar's understanding of a *Bhikku* and the *Sangha* is rigid, for "Great responsibility lies on the shoulders of the *Bhikkus,* if this attempt at the revival of Buddhism is to be a success. They must be more active than they have been. They must come out of their shell and be in the front rank of the fighting forces[19]". The main responsibility of the *Bhikku* is conversion. At the same time, like the Buddha who commissioned his disciples (*Parivrajakas*), to go forth to liberate people—to teach people the path of *Nibbana,* Ambedkar too asks the new converts to do the same. Here Ambedkar adds that every Buddhist has the right to initiate others, to go forth with the message of the Buddha, to go forth to liberate people as there were no Bhikkus in this country to do this work. We note that at the time of his own conversion, Ambedkar took the 'three refuges and five precepts'—the symbolic acceptance of

Buddhism—from the then senior-most monk in India; but right in his presence and in the presence of many other monks, he administered the same to the mass that had assembled to embrace Buddhism. This he did *himself,* to assert the right to initiate any one into Buddhism by a *layman*. Therefore what could have been a great ritual conducted by a Buddhist clergy as a Ritual, is now conducted as a *Ceremony* by either monk (*Bhikku*) or a layman (*Upasana*). When the most important event for a Buddhist—*Diksha*—should have been a ritual is not identified as one, it could be deemed only a ceremony. This being so, the rest of the events in the life of a Neo-Buddhist, Christening or marriage, they all become functions or ceremonies only.

Hence in Neo-Buddhism there is no 'Ritual' (*Samskara*) at all. There are only ceremonies and festivals.

REFERENCES

1. Ambedkar, Dr. B.R., *Buddha and His Dhamma,* pp. 322-23, vss. 2, 3, 7.
2. *Ibid.,* pp. 355-56.
3. *Ibid.,* p. 357, vs. iff.
4. *Ibid.,* p. 359, vs. iff.
5. *Ibid.,* pp. 359-61.
6. *Ibid.,* pp. 361-62.
7. *Ibid.,* pp. 364-66.
8. *Ibid.,* pp. 366-67.
9. *Ibid.,* pp. 367-68.
10. *Ibid.,* pp. 368-69.
11. *Ibid.,* pp. 370-71.

12. *Ambedkar, op. cit.*, pp. 370-71.
13. *Ibid.*, pp. 371-72.
14. *Ibid.*, pp. 383-84.
15. *Ibid.*, p. 385.
16. *Ibid.*, p. 386.
17. *Ibid.*, pp. 392-93.
18. *Ibid.*, p. 121, vs. 14.
19. Sangharakshita, *op. cit.*, p. 16.

7

NEO-BUDDHISM AND SOME WESTERN THINKERS

NEO-BUDDHISM AND THE ECONOMIC THOUGHTS OF ROBERT BALDWIN

The contribution of a few Western thinkers has influenced many scholars and statesmen all over the world. Emile Durkheim, Mex Weber and Robert Baldwin are three among them. Seldom we get to apply the thoughts of eminent scholars to specific societies or persons as universal to particular. Here we would see relevance of these three to Ambedkar and the Neo-Buddhist Movement.

K.S. Bharathi, a scholar on Gandhian thought, in his book *Foundations of Ambedkar Thought* says that Ambedkar was influenced by many; e.g., Ramji Sakpal (his father), Mahatma Jyoti Rao Phooley, Ranade and Gandhi—among Indians and Prof. John Dewey Ambedkar's Professor at

Columbia—Karl Marx, J.S. Mill, among foreigners.[1] It is difficult to say if Ambedkar's thoughts were influenced by his voracious reading of social scientists like (French) Emile Durkheim, (German) Max Weber and (American Economist) Robert E. Baldwin, whose thoughts seem to anticipate and ratify Ambedkar's thoughts, amazingly and strikingly. The thoughts of Durkheim, Weber and Baldwin appear to have direct connotation to the Neo-Buddhist movement. Let us begin with Robert E. Baldwin.

Baldwin fully vindicates Ambedkar's position as he says: "post-war growth experience in the developing countries has convinced more and more development economists that the Agricultural and Industrial sectors must expand side-by-side, if growth is to be more than the establishment of a few flashy industries or the creation of an agricultural surplus that soon disappears into larger rural population".[2] Ambedkar was a development economist. He was against complete state monopoly of economy (differing from communism). He favoured state ownership in the fields of insurance, industry and agricultural land. He believed that India should industrialise or she would perish. Private enterprise cannot industrialise Indian socio-economy and if it would, it would produce those inequalities of wealth which private capitalism has produced in European countries.

Ambedkar's economic thoughts are well-defined and precise. How correct is Baldwin's analysis that agricultural and industrial sectors must expand side-by-side, if growth is to be more than the establishment of a few flashy industries or creations of an agricultural surplus....! As we watch the planning policy of the Indian Government giving great emphasis on agricultural and industrial sectors, with banking advances to the needy private enterpreneurs but holding in its hands on major industries, we see the progress of India in both agricultural and industrial sectors have been tremendous; call it Green Revolution in agriculture or

White Revolution in dairy industry, public sector undertakings in heavy engineering are responsible for job opportunities for millions of people. This also gives opportunities for the Mahars as well as other untouchables for change of profession by choice and as such, breaks the monotony of sticking to ancestral professions even though talents for a change in vocation of an 'untouchable' individual is well-evidenced. Ahir rightly says: "the post-independence efforts create a welfare-state through planned economic development and industrialisation are more akin to the ideas of Ambedkar..."[3] This augurs well with Emile Durkheim's theory of education for vocation, about which we will be discussing in the coming section. All the more now, Neo-Buddhists, with their separate identity, can opt for change in vocation of their choice in the fields of agricultural and other industries. There are 'Neo-Buddhist' enterpreneurs who are either small-scale industrialists or employees of big industrial houses. The country progresses, the ex-lowliest in the caste system, as Buddhists (or Buddhist sympathisers), progress too. Baldwin's analysis helps us to impartially evaluate Ambedkar's vision for India and for the lowliest community among the lowly.

We would examine some of Baldwin's theories which appear to reflect the woes and the eventual transition of 'ex-touchables'. Baldwin had said, "Individuals who have lost status and respect become frustrated and angry, but are powerless to affect society's attitude to them..."[4] Baldwin wrote this theory with the American peasant-based society in mind. But if we relate it to the socially down-trodden communities in India, like the untouchables, Baldwin's theory become relevant to Ambedkar. Society is after all a magnified individual. We may say that the untouchables are forced to flee and run away,...... like the cats, or bark in a muffled tone like a beaten dog? In the case of 'untouchables', it is not mere losing of status and respect, which Baldwin refers to, but being born without either of these.

Baldwin has reflected a real situation. But what is the way out? His theory is, as the title of his book suggests, *Economic Development and Growth* and this is directly related to sociological factors. He posits a theory which seems to directly and positively pointing to Ambedkar; he says: "One of the most interesting and ambitious current lines of thought concerning the role of non-economic factors in development focuses upon the emergence of the 'creative' or 'achieving' type of personality. Those who possess this personality seem to initiate economic motivation and progress".[5] History reveals emergence of such 'creative' or 'achieving' types from time-to-time. Why current lines of thought in non-economic roles? Such realities have been in the past too. Buddha rebelled against Brahminism, Martin Luther King, Jr., rebelled in the USA against apartheid in recent times and Dr. Nelson Mandela in our times. There have been a dozen of personalities from spiritual to sociological roles all over the world—as 'achievers', apart from the countless 'attempters' as reformers all over the world. Limiting ourselves to the Indian context and converging further into the socio-religious aspect exclusively, we may stress that there have been hundreds of social reformers who attempted in this area.

The 'creative' and 'achieving' personality type described by Baldwin fits Dr. Ambedkar perfectly. Safely it could be surmised that Ambedkar could 'achieve' whatever he did, as he was 'creative' in this thinking. Ambedkar, by tradition, would have passed off as a docile, volatile, capricious, and callous as most of the menials are. If Ambedkar stands in the world esteem like Colossus, it is by dint of iron-will, indomitable spirit and intense desire to 'achieve' (Baldwin). Every step that he trod, he faced obstacles and opposition. But for his 'elon-vit-al'(as expounded by Bergson) casteism would have crippled him too. He was manoeuvring his moves one after another towards a clearly defined objective to the cause of removal of untouchability and alleviation as well as amelioration of the plight of the untouchables; whatever else he did they were incidental or additional because he was a creative thinker. We may quote Ahir again as he compares the contribution of the earlier social reformers with Ambedkar: "....Ambedkar, for the first time, evolved another method of self-development, self-reliance and direction by the untouchables themselves. He made these unfortunate classes conscious of their miserable condition and shook them out of their age-old lethargy and in-action. Verily, the spirit of courage, boldness and self-respect among the ex-untouchables of India are the gift of Ambedkar"[6].

The untouchables—the Mahars—were deemed to have become ex-untouchables by becoming Buddhists and as followers of Buddhism propounded by Dr. Ambedkar, they were to be identified as Neo-Buddhists. What does this change imply in terms of economic growth of that community? Baldwin suggests a contrasting comparison between Karl Marx and Max Weber, the two great German thinkers: "Marx is one who goes beyond the traditional boundaries of economics in analysing the growth process. However, even though economic change involves such socio-political phenomena as the class-struggle, the basic direction of causality in the Marxian System still proceeds from economic factors to cultural conditions. Max Weber is an example of a writer who would reverse this causality...."[7] A simplified version of this theory is: "to him (Marx), a change in economic and political conditions may also lead to a social change. Max Weber establishes a reverse causality".[8] In other words, Baldwin presents a striking and contradicting contrast in the theories of Marx and Weber. Whereas economic growth may lead to a social change in the Marxian system (i.e. Communism) for an individual in the society or a social group, for Max Weber, social change in an individual or group would lead to economic development of that individual or group. This seems to be very valid in the case of the untouchables who opted out of Hindu fold to become Buddhists and thus secured a separate identity for themselves as Neo-Buddhists. By getting separate identity, this community has become a new social group or a society by itself and from this new point their economic prosperity gets counted. But does this happen overnight? It is, assuredly, a slow process but yet a steady one.

Baldwin incorporates the view of sociologist W.W. Rolston and says: "There are five stages of economic growth, namely, the traditional society, pre-conditions for take off, drive to maturity and the age of high mass consumption".[9] The growth of any society is assumed to be beginning from zero level and grows from that level to `high mass consumption'.

We will relate the growth of ex-Mahars to the nascent Neo-Buddhists of 1956, who 'took off' into growth potential. But before 'taking off', what was that society? We had seen various modes of humiliations, injustices for the 'untouchables' were subjected to, from which Dr. Ambedkar, after bitter experiences, emerged out as a 'creative' and 'achieving' personality type declaring, as we have noted earlier that it was his birthright to lead a human and honourable life. It was not a mere statement but was based on pangs of sufferings. The untouchables were denied the basic human rights due to the existence of horrible disabilities. The census of 1931 mentioned five categories of disabilities which were put in enjoyment of the human rights by the untouchables:

(1) Obstacles in the way of using public institutions or amenities such as schools, wells or bathing places;

(2) Prohibition on entry into Hindu temples or in some cases, on the use of burning ghats;

(3) Refusing to render them service on caste grounds, e.g., barbers, tailors or washermen;

(4) Refusing to take water from them; and

(5) Pollution by contact or proximity.[10]

These disabilities and social situation may be construed as 'the traditional society' suggested by W.W. Rolston and developed by Robert Baldwin, with respect to Mahar community before becoming Neo-Buddhists.

The next stage of Rolston's perception was 'preconditions for take off'. Thus, when we apply this to the Neo-Buddhists before they become so, it is to be considered in the light of Baldwin's analysis as non-economic and economic stages. What was the plight of the Mahars in the non-economic and economic arena? Socially, they were living a miserable life; intellectually, the very fact that Ambedkar's passing the Matriculation as the first-ever Mahar to achieve this was celebrated by the community as a whole; economically they were, needless to mention, totally backward. Poverty was their way of life, leave alone below-poverty line; spiritually, they were denied the privileges of worshipping in a public temple like other superior castes.

What would be, then, the 'take off' stage for the Mahars? It would be easily comparable to Israelites going out of the land of Egypt to an unknown land of Canaan, in the history of Judaism (and Dr. Ambedkar rightly compared himself with Moses, the leader).[11] Judaistic history recorded (as also recorded in the *Bible*, and passively in the history of the world), that the Israelites were slaves under the Pharoas of Egypt for nearly four hundred years, were led out of Egypt by Moses into the land of Canaan where they started all afresh. According to the *Bible*, the history of Israel starts with Abraham as the father of the posterity which came to be called as Israelites, who prospered even as nomads until they settled down in Egypt and prospered there more than the local Egyptians. They were gradually enslaved and remained slaves until they were delivered out of the hands of the Pharoah then, by Moses. This tribe, over the years, went on to become a powerful kingdom founded by Saul, consolidated by David and fortified by Solomon. Similarly going back to the Mahars, would it be wrong to say that they have 'taken off' all afresh by relinquishing the Hindu fold, and embracing Buddhism—thus becoming Neo-Buddhists. Starting with nothing in the economic, social, spiritual and intellectual fields, this socially 'enslaved' society may well be deemed to have 'emancipated' themselves for a fine 'take-off'—they may one day fly as eagles.

The next stage is suggested as 'drive to maturity' stage. The social change among the Mahars is a reality. They are now reckoned as one among the millions of Buddhist fraternity all over the world. First and foremost, what they acquired by the change of religion is spiritual outlet in the spirit of liberty, equality and justice. Would they grow into spiritual and mundane maturity? Would it be possible for them to shun the traditions and customs that they were associated with while in Hinduism, what Gandhiji referred to as 'changing the cloak'? Even after nearly four decades of the first mass conversions in 1956, conversions are still taking place. Some of the 'Untouchable' Hindus are remaining as 'Dalit' Hindus, with the desire for conversion hovering around them always. The studies that were conducted by various individuals and agencies (Ref. Chapter VIII) indicate that the very fact that the downtrodden ex-untouchables have shed their superstitions is a pointer that they are on a 'drive to maturity'. That they have shunned their 'inferiority complex' is another pointer towards 'drive to maturity' socially. The observations of this author affirm a 'drive to maturity' in the field on education too. In every aspect desirable in a welfare society it can be emphatically asserted that the Neo-Buddhists are now in a stage of 'drive to maturity' as defined by Rolston and amplified by Baldwin. This is a growing stage in which the Mahars-turned-Buddhists are now in with growth potential and plentiful. While Baldwin's theory is limited only to economic growth and development of a traditional society, we can extend it to an all-round growth of the Neo-Buddhists on the whole. The newly-found social identity of the Neo-Buddhists is pointedly relative to their economic growth and prosperity. The possibilities for growth in other avenues of life also broaden and brighten.

The final stage of 'the age of high mass consumption' is for realisation in the years and decades to come as far as the Neo-Buddhists are concerned. The rapidity of the growth as observed in the Neo-Buddhist community is indeed great. Of course, the centrifugal force was the immortal Dr. Babasaheb Ambedkar. This movement has caused so much of interest amongst the sociologists and scholars that a constant and continuous study is on the move from all aspects.

NEO-BUDDHISM AND MAX WEBER

Max Weber has written on sociology, politics and religion and has, interestingly, written on Hinduism too. He lived through the latter half of the nineteenth century to the first quarter of this century and his writings are read with respect all over the world. A while ago, we saw his ability to reverse Karl Marx's prescription for economic growth as analysed by Robert Baldwin. The thesis of Weber in the light of Baldwin's analysis has to be examined as it appears pertinent to our study.

Max Weber was well-acquainted with all the systems of the world, ranging from spiritualism to communism. His analysis of the problems relating to caste and how this factor affected India is indeed a study by itself. But we would adapt what seems relevant and pertinent to our analysis and then would try and analyse his thoughts.

To begin with, Max Weber's assessment of Hinduism is very interesting. He states: "Hinduism is an eclectic and tolerant religion: It is possible to be a devout Hindu and yet to accept highly important and most characteristic doctrines which every denominational Christian would consider exclusively his own".[12] How true this statement is, specially seen in the life of saints like Ramakrishna Paramahamsa! Thus Weber's analysis of Hinduism is true to the core. There are many schools of thought within Indian philosophy—orthodox and heterodox and all the adherents of these schools are generally classified as Hindus; even among the orthodox, one system of Indian philosophy does not agree with another.

Another aspect of Weber's analysis of Hinduism is his opinion about 'Karma'. "The doctrine of Karma, according to him, represents the most consistent theodicy ever produced in history".[13] Because of it, Giddens interprets Weber to say, adapting a slogan from the communist manifesto, the Hindu of the lowest caste can 'win the world'.[14] Weber had understood the tenets of Karma and rebirth and so he could justly borrow the communist slogan to achieve something which is impossible. Hindu theodicy, being the factors relating to immortality of the soul and Divine justice, is lauded by Max Weber. But what has he to say about caste? The following quotation is illuminating: "The emergence of caste system entirely displaced other organisations; in part, it crippled them; it prevented them from attaining any considerable importance".[15]

If an Indian had written this passage, the first half of eulogy would be well taken and the second half rejected as prejudiced and biased. It may be mentioned here that when Ambedkar was about to deliver an address, the quint essence of which was more or less the same, at Jat-Pat-Todak Mandal Conference at Lahore in 1936, the whole Conference was cancelled stating that the views expressed in the speech would be unbearable to the Conference. Max Weber holds that the emergence of the Caste System:

(1) prevented effectively any further economic development comparable to what was taking shape in Europe;

(2) crippled them (progress);

(3) prevented considerable importance to be attained.

Weber had said so decades before Ambedkar. Max Weber's analysis is very right and relevant to the Mahars before they became Buddhists. That they have come out of this caste-structure of Hinduism is to say that they have literally broken the fetters that had crippled them for ages. Having broken their fetters, they are free people, but with a new identity. With this new identity, they have 'taken off' as a society. Having secured this identity they have a social standing, not theirs hitherto. But henceforth, with their new formed social standing, is their spiritual progress and mundane prosperity a possibility? Yes, they have already embraced a faith that gives them not only a social status, but also, as such, they are a new community of believers in common brotherhood—a fraternity; so also, their mundane prosperity—their economic growth and development is a possibility. The latter assertion is the theory of Max Weber, which we had touched upon a while ago. We have seen, how Baldwin compares the theories of Karl Marx and Max Weber. For Marx, the economic development of a society is related to the cultural setting of that society. But in Weber, it is a reverse causality— the cultural setting of the society is related to its economic development. Max Weber directly illustrates his thesis with Calvinistic idea of thrift. Weber includes Baptists and Methodists too. These Protestant denominations of Christianity are against blind following of the mass to the dictates of papacy. Religious values lead to economic growth and development. Calvinism emphasises perseverance and thrift. The discipline of Methodist Church fosters, as religious persons, values like punctuality, thrift, hard and itenerant work and deplores all that is vain; so also does the Baptist denomination. The followers of these denominations, in the opinion of Max Weber (and very truly so), have attained such economic growth that their pattern of economic standards have been fostered capitalist form of society in the West. The idea of 'saving' in these denominations in the West have cultivated a strong and formidable funding, that their value of sharing is routed to the needy all over the world. Max Weber's analysis is opposed to the Marxian axioms, which deprives individual of his right to choose as everything is the property of State.

Relating this theory to the Neo-Buddhists of today, it can be emphatically asserted that this theory is the truth behind the progress that is seen in the Neo-Buddhist community. Max Weber's assertion emenates from his observation of the Christian circles he has been in. In a multicultural set-up like the one which is existing in India today, every community outside ex-Hindu fold is 'endogamy' and all that is within this broad group is growing and prospering and when Ambedkar says "endogamy is the only characteristic that is peculiar in caste",[16] we may underscore Max Weber to say that caste has crippled India's progress by making Hindu society a static one ever since caste took its firm root in the society, more specially so, when we consider the fate of the untouchables over the centuries.

In the speech prior to conversion in 1956 Ambedkar said: "I know myself what sort of hardships the poor have to bear. We must launch our struggle keeping in view the economic aspects and I am not against this idea. We should progress economically too and endeavour to become independent".[17] What then, would be the scope of the economic growth of the Neo-Buddhists? If Max Weber has seen Calvanists, Baptists and Methodists and their fixation on work and thrift. they were based on piety. We can safely relate it to the Neo-Buddhists too. Though there is no God in Neo-Buddhism and therefore no piety, in place of God there is morality. Buddhist principles of living are based on utter simplicity. Ambedkar's constant exhortations to his followers have been `struggle', 'fight for your rights', `Don't waste any more (time)', and `justice'. Religious values are resonant with Buddhist ethics. We may say that this Neo-Buddhist ethics with its emphasis on work and thrift is likely to become the crucial element accounting for the success of Indian socialist development.

We may conclude that Max Weber's analysis of caste, and his indictment on this system, though much milder than Dr. Ambedkar's, are very relevant and refreshing for understanding the Mahars. His theory that religion (or religious values) in its cultural setting in a society is related to (or causes) economic growth and development should be taken as a prophesy with regard to the Neo-Buddhists.

NEO-BUDDHISM AND EMILE DURKHEIM

1. Concept of Liberation

The celebrated French sociologist of Jewish origin Emile Durkheim was the contemporary of Max Weber. Unlike Weber he was an unbeliever and therefore his analysis of religion was impersonal and rationalistic. The common bond between them, in addition to many others, was their rational approach to the Communist doctrine. They wrote differing with Communist ideology. A brief quote by Anthony Giddens would introduce the relevance of Durkheim to our study: "Durkheim began his intellectual career with the attempt to found a `Science of Morality'. This endeavour led him to sociology, which was to provide a method for such a science. But the formulation of that method in turn led him back to morality, since the moral character of social facts is their distinguishing feature"[18].

Ambedkar emphasises the place of morality in religion (*Dhamma)* and devotes for that the entire Section III of

Part V in *Buddha and His Dhamma*. As noted in Buddhism, there is no God, hence morality takes the place of religion. We may recall his dictum "In *Dhamma*, morality is God and God is morality". For Durkheim too, morality takes a unique place.

We have seen the fate of the Mahar community as untouchables in the Indian society. Why were they conditioned into submission for ages, and what is the difference in their community out of that state of submission in terms of the thinking of sociologists like Emile Durkheim? What would have been their status, had they continued to be in that state of submission even for ages to come within that society? Anthony Giddens analyses Durkheim in nutshell and ends with a quote from Durkheim himself: "... One dimension in which society has a liberating effect is in freeing man from subjection to the world of nature, in delivering him from blind unthinking physical forces! His submission to society is the condition of this liberation. In the most simple forms of society, this submission is more or less total. The level of individuality and autonomy of action are low. In these societies, the simplicity of moral behaviour makes it easy to transform such behaviour into habits, mechanically carried out ... custom and tradition have such power and prestige as to leave no place for reasoning and questioning".[19]

The aforesaid passage seems to fit into the Indian society, specially the hitherto submissive Mahar society. As rightly pointed out by Durkheim,"the level of individuality and autonomy of action are low", not only in most simple forms of society, as suggested by Durkheim, but also in a complexed form of Indian, more appropriately, Hindu society.

Durkheim's analysis of society is remarkable when he says that, as noted above, 'one dimension in which society has a liberating effect is in freeing man from subjection to the world of nature, in delivering him from blind unthinking physical forces. When this is applied to the Mahars, the whole society around it may be construed as 'the society' and it has a liberating effect from subjection to the world of 'untouchability centred nature' and 'the society' comprising enlightened individuals from the upper castes (like Dr. Ambedkar's Brahmin teacher Ambedkar Kaluskar and the Maharajas of Baroda and Kolhapore and from the lowest like Ambedkar himself)—has liberating effect from irrational and egoistic individuals.

For Durkheim, "man is necessarily a mixed and contradictory being".[20] To the question "can acts which are purely egoistic, (i.e., oriented wholly to the self) have moral character?" Durkheim said that "they cannot; self interest is logically distinct from moral conduct".[21] We may surmise that the 'Hindu society', comprising egoistic individuals as to ensure servitude from the untouchables has been reduced to immorality; though the 'Hindu religion' may be, as Gandhiji interpreted, was (to use the title of an earlier work of Emile Durkheim), 'division of labour'. The Hindu society, we may infer, had deviated from the 'division of labour' to strictly enforce 'division of castes' and hence become decadent and immoral. It must be noted that "Egoism and moral character are discrete and in chronic potential opposition".[22] Hence a situation arose that the Mahars opted, under the leadership of Ambedkar, to leave the Hindu society. Thus, the common usage of Neo-Buddhists, that they were liberated from hell, seems to be in line with Durkheim's thinking.

It is Buddhism, where *Dhamma* and morality are synonymous terms. In choosing Buddhism, as their way of life, the Mahars adopted for themselves a religion which has in it highest standards of moral codes. Their coming out of the Hindu fold was to seek 'an autonomous and satisfying human experience'and they have it now in full and in abundance.

2. From Theism to Neo-Theism

By embracing Buddhism, the Mahar social group have renounced theism and taken to a religion of atheism. But in doing so, the morality of the Mahars has been set to higher and more desirable standard, deviating into a system devoid of Theology. The Buddhist ethics forbids intoxicants; teaches human equality; insists on non-violence; encourages knowledge of all in all areas; is rational and scientific in its approach to the problems of life. The religious system is rational and rationality justifies morality. The *Dhamma* is equated with morality. In a system without Theology, what Durkheim says seems to hold good that religion (the *Dhamma*) and morality cannot be separated; they are inseparable. The viewpoint of Durkheim with regard to Neo-Buddhists is valid and morality has the place of God, which the Mahars were used to worshipping. We may conclude that in Neo-Buddhism there should be no more worshipping of any Hindu deity; morality cannot be 'worshipped' as such, but may be 'adored' for its values and ideals of 'moral individualism'. We must note that in the twenty-two vows, pronouns of first person 'I' were used by Ambedkar and are now used in all initiation ceremonies to eliminate worshipping.

Now let us see a definition of 'Society' by Durkheim, which is important to us. He said, "If we cannot be bound by duty to conscious beings and we have eliminated the individual, there remains as the only other possible object of moral activity the *Sui generis* collective being founded by the plurality of individuals associated to form a group ... we arrive then at the conclusion that society is a moral being, qualitatively different from the individuals it comprises and from the aggregation it derives".[23]

When Durkheim says, 'duty to conscious beings', he refers to Kant's idea of duty. More elaboration of Kant's dictum and Durkheim's development on that is not warranted here, and suffice it would to say that "Duty, the Kantian imperative, is only one abstract aspect of moral reality",[24] and Durkheim emphasized that "the imperative character of moral acts is not exhausted by negative sanctions violation of a moral rule by the Kantian idea of duty ... for the negative sanctions associated with moral rules are complimented by positive ones, those of praise, honour, etc., which derive from conformity to moral norms and which make moral conduct satisfying or fulfilling.... In some cases duty pre-ponderates; in other instances the opposite applies ..."[25] This, we can say, leads us to assume that we cannot be bound by duty to conscious beings and similarly considerations of 'individuals'could be underscored. Therefore, what was left as the object of moral activity is that individuals become a collective mass to form a 'group'. Thus a society is formed as such. Earlier Durkheim had said, "these interwing facets of moral codes (positive and negative) are most clearly exemplified by religion ..."[26] Ambedkar's analysis of this duality within the light of the Buddha's teachings is: "The answer which the Buddha gave to the question, How is moral order maintained? ...'it is the *Kamma Niyam* and not God which maintains the moral order in the universe' ... The moral order of the Universe may be good or bad. But according to the Buddha the moral order rests on man and on nobody else. *Kamma* means action and *vipaku* is its effect. If the moral order is bad, it is because man does *akusala* (bad) *kamma*. If the moral order is good, it is because man does *kusala* (good) *kamma* ... No one could fail to benefit by the good effects of *kusala kamma* and no one could escape the evil effects of *akusala kamma*".[27] The moral activity of a group, in other words, is exemplified by religion.

Now, to take up the second half the quote mentioned earlier, "we arrive then at that...Society is a moral being...." It (the society) is qualitatively different from its member individuals or the membership en masse. In Durkheim's analysis society is personified as a moral being, not by quantity at all, but differing by quality of the individual or the mass it comprises. Thus morality is equated with society.

Relating this to the Neo-Buddhists, if *Dhamma* is morality , and if Durkheim could establish that 'Society' is a moral being, there seems to be a unique identity for the Neo-Buddhist society in the sense that 'God is morality', 'Society is morality' and '*Dhamma* is morality'. Ambedkar had said: "... Morality is *Dhamma* and *Dhamma* is Morality. In other words, *Dhamma* takes the place of God although there is no God in *Dhamma* ... Morality is the essence of *Dhamma*. Without it there is no *Dhamma*. Morality arises from the direct necessity for man to love man. It does not require the sanction of God. It is not to please God that man has to be moral. It is for his own good that man has to love man".[28] The object of moral activity is to form a good society. Morality is the sum and substance of Neo-Buddhism. This moral activity of millions becoming Buddhists has led into forming a group, a society. Now the ex-untouchable Mahars have a new society on the basis of the tenets of Buddhism and hence they have a new identity for themselves. We can, therefore say, that this 'Religion' gives an identity to the converted Mahars. The moral standards are not to be compromised with the studying of the individuals converted, but set above their human limitations.

Another theory of Durkheim seems to be very relevant in the belief of the Neo-Buddhists and Dr. Ambedkar himself, particularly, in the dualism of soul and body. Durkheim asserts that body and soul are in conflict with each other, leave alone they being different. Durkheim says that soul living in body is symbolic of this dualism. Sensation and sensory needs of the body are in tension with 'conceptual thought' on the one hand and moral activity on the other. Here appears to be a dogma which *prima facie* does not fit into the belief of Buddhism in general and Neo-Buddhism in particular. The Neo-Buddhist belief is that there is soul, while they (Ambedkarites) believe in the mind and body: "The Buddha was not an eternalist. For it involved a belief in the existence of a separate immortal soul to which he was opposed... He believed in the regeneration of matter and not in the rebirth of the soul"[29]. On mind and its relation to morality Ambedkar quotes the Buddha: "...the mind is the master, the mind is the cause. If in the midst of the mind, there are evil thoughts, the words are evil, the deeds are evil... If in the mind there are good thoughts, then the words are good and the deeds are good..."[30] To adapt the theory of Durkheim, while relating to morality and system of religious thought, we have to replace 'soul' with 'mind'. Similarly, when we replace 'soul' with 'mind' in Neo-Buddhism, the theory of Durkheim becomes relevant. Morality is a 'disinterested activity' and as much as it would be universalised, it could be individualised too; this could be magnified somewhat to a corporate society as well. The tension between the body and mind is real in human personality in a 'Neo-Buddhist' society. All moral acts involve some element and some degree of self-sacrifice. This statement becomes true in the case of Dr. Ambedkar, whose moral standing has never been in question.

'Education' was another major concern for Dr. Ambedkar and he often cited his miserable experiences as poor Mahar boy at school. Durkheim, in his treatise on education, dwells at length on education of young children. Durkheim's views are: "Education varies between different strata within society: In types of society prior to modern times,2 literary and other educational arts have been the prerogative of small elite groups... there still are major differences between the classes in terms of character and level of the formal education typically enjoyed... the education children receive should no longer be determined by the class position into which they happen to be born".[31] How true these observations are with regard to the fate of the untouchables, until untouchability was abolished by law and educational opportunities were given to the students belonging to the untouchable communities, like the Mahars.

As Durkheim had anticipated, the theistic contention of education with regard to casteism in India, has now virtually disappeared. The division of castes have been replaced by the concept of division of labour and along with it the modern education system, on principles—to say the least—has begun to transmit secular values and codes of conduct relevant to the Indian society. This has benefited the Neo-Buddhist society to a considerable extent.

Another factor that Durkheim brings to notice of the reader is about a teacher; "...The teacher must also establish himself as a moral exampler who conditions the child's behaviour through his demeanour as well as through public instruction".[32] This, if we broaden the aspects of any moral teacher, it would exemplify Dr. Ambedkar as an ideal teacher.

Durkheim's most celebrated book is *The Elementary Forms of Religious Life.* In that he traces the history of religion beginning with Australian totemism. He had, in that work, limited himself to the development of religion.

We may point out another facet of Durkheim's analysis of religion in the light of what Giddens has to interpret: "The notion of evolutionary differentiation upon which Durkheim relied in his work meant he had no qualms in holding that simplest form of religion must be found in the simplest form of society".[33] Neo-Buddhism is absolutely simple, that we may even venture to say `Buddhism made simple'. There is no voluminous treatises to read, no rituals associated with it at all, there is no eminence of clergy over the laity. The entire Buddhist texts have been abridged into one handy book (though somewhat large in size)—*Buddha and His Dhamma*. The only ritual or ceremony associated with it, as Ambedkar had done, was the initiation ceremony at the time of conversion of an individual into Buddhism.

What is the Neo-Buddhist society, if not a simple society as such? The Mahars were an untouchable lot, and simplicity was their way of life. Though they have embraced Buddhism en masse, those who have, yet they form of simple society in which they live as part of a wider and complexed society. It won't be wrong to say, that in today's context, it is the simplest type of society.

In Durkheim's words: "There can be no society which does not feel the need of upholding and reaffirming at regular intervals, the collective sentiments and the collective ideas which give it its unity and individuality".[34] The Neo-Buddhist movement is such a society and its spirit is followed up by the Dalit movement. For Ambedkar, morality is the ultimate reality of the *Dhamma* and his belief in Buddhism is based on what can be cognised by scientific truth and verified. It is fascinating to note Ambedkar's selection of Buddhism as his religion of choice on the basis of morality and science and Durkheim's emphasis on these two, to compliment each other.

Thus, in the aforesaid analysis, most of Durkheim's philosophy of religion, education and sociology, seems to go well to re-interpret various aspects of Neo-Buddhism.

REFERENCES

1. Cf. Bharathi, K.S. *Foundations of Ambedkar Thought*, Dattsons, Nagpur, 1990, pp. 41-61.
2. Baldwin, Robert E., *Economic Development and Growth*. John Wiley & Sons Inc., New York, 1966, p. 70.
3. Ahir, D.C., *Gandhi and Ambedkar*, p. 75.
4. Baldwin, Robert E., *op. cit.*, p. 63.
5. *Ibid.*, p. 62.
6. Ahir, D.C., *op. cit.*, p. 52.
7. Baldwin, Robert E., *op. cit.*, pp. 61-62.
8. Pande, G.C. & Pandey, P.C., *Social Anatomy of Economic Growth*, Anmol Publications, New Delhi, 1990, p. 31.
9. Baldwin, Robert, E., *op. cit.*, p. 67.
10. Cf. Lokhande, Prof., G.S., *Dr. Babasaheb Ambedkar on the Hindu Static Society*, "Deep", Nagpur, December 1967, p. 7.
11. Exodus : Chapter 12.
12. Cf. Giddens, Anthony, *Capitalism and Modern Social Theory: An Analysis of the Writings of Marx, Durkheim and Max Weber*, Cambridge University Press, Cambridge, 1979, p. 172.
13. Weber, Max, *The Religion of India*, The Free Press, New York, 1967, p. 121.
14. Giddens, Anthony, *op. cit.*, p. 113.
15. Weber, Max, *op. cit.*, p. 34.
16. Ambedkar, *Castes in India*, Bheem Patrika Publications, Jalandhar, p. 8.
17. *Ambedkar's Patriotic Call*, p. 5.
18. Giddens, Anthony, *Durkheim*, William Collins Sons & Co. Ltd. Glassow, 1978, p. 63.
19. *Ibid.*, pp. 70-71.
20. *Ibid.*, p. 69.
21. *Ibid.*, p. 66.
22. *Ibid.*, pp. 68-69.
23. *Ibid.*, p. 67.
24. *Ibid.*, p. 65.
25. *Ibid.*, p. 65.
26. *Ibid.*, p. 66.
27. Ambedkar, Dr. B.R., *Buddha and His Dhamma*, p. 243.
28. *Ibid.*, pp. 322-23.
29. *Ibid.*, pp. 329-32.

30. Ambedkar, Dr. B.R., *Buddha and His Dhamma*, p. 282.
31. Giddens, Anthony, *Durkheim*, p. 72.
32. *Ibid.*, p. 86.
33. *Ibid.*, p. 86.
34. *Ibid.*, p. 99.

8

IMPACT OF NEO-BUDDHISM IN INDIA AND ABROAD

In this chapter we are considering the impact of Neo-Buddhism at home and abroad. We have hitherto seen the various aspects of Neo-Buddhism from a few possible angles, though briefly. We ought to study what influence Neo-Buddhism, as a socio-religious movement, wields over at home and its impact abroad.

ON THE NEO-BUDDHISTS.

When we say Neo-Buddhists, here we mainly refer to the first batch of Mahars who converted themselves into Buddhism along with Ambedkar in 1956, at Nagpur and their progeny. The subsequent converts in Maharashtra and other parts of India, could also be broadly included in this category.

A survey that was conducted by the Gokhale Institute of Research, Poona, in 1962 at Bombay to ascertain the impact of the change of religion by the Scheduled Castes. The Researchers reported the impact on the Scheduled Castes as 'tremendous'. The report further opined that the Scheduled Caste people have now become one and are very much united. They are trying to establish a casteless society on the principles of Buddhism. They are extremely proud of Buddhism. They are leading a dignified and honourable life in the society. The reservation today in education, employment, Legislative Assemblies, and Parliament will positively disappear after sometime, but the Buddhists as a group will remain and fight for their own rights as a minority community.[1]

The impact of Buddha's teachings was studied by Arun Siddhu in 1978. His report revealed that:

(a) The ex-untouchables got rid of their inferiority complex; they have a fresh identity and a new acquired confidence. What is more, the youth among them have completely shed superstitions;....

(b) There is a new cultural and social renaissance which has transformed the youth ... only hard work, education and a rational approach would bring progress, they believe;

(c) As far as the economic status is concerned there is only a marginal change among the newly educated Buddhists... By and large they have remained economically at the same level at which they were before conversion. But the radical transition from blind faith to rationalism has given rise to tremendous hunger for education and knowledge among the Buddhist youth. This holds the key to their economic progress.[2]

(We must note here that Max Weber's theory that change in cultural setting leads to economic prosperity is vindicated by the above paragraph.)

In 1979, this author conducted a survey on the Neo-Buddhists at Nagpur. Some of the findings are as follows: (15 select respondents out of 30; total forms distributed 50.)

General

I. Age group: 30-50 years.

II. Religious Status: Neo-Buddhists by *conversion* (of all).

III. Education: B.E.—1 (Electrical Engineer)

(i) at Degree B.Sc., D.M.A.—1 (Medical level Representative)

B.Com. —3 }
B.A. —3 } Government employees
B.Sc. —1 }
(Agriculture)

(ii) Post-Graduates: M.A. 2
M.Com. 1
M.A.(Eco), M.A.(Mar), B.J., LL.B—1
M.A.(His), M.A.(Pol. Sc.) LL.B, B.Ed.—1
M.A.(Pol.Sc.), M.A.(Socio), LL.B—1

Of the 15-case study material, only *two* had answered that changing religion has given them new status *financially*; The other 12 had said *No*; One said *Not fully*. All the 15 persons to the question whether change of religion helped socially, responded that socially the change of religion has helped them.

To the question, 'if a convert, why', replies were: (select 10).

(i) To give up caste names which denotes 'untouchable' in Hindu religion.

(ii) To believe in human dignity; not to believe in an invisible God.

(iii) Hinduism is inhuman, unscientific; conduct stand for liberation of man.

(iv) 'I was innocent at the time of conversion (1956). But along with parents I was converted'.

(v) Came out of Hindu religion which treats the untouchables as sub-human; self-respect.

(vi) Having wholehearted faith in Dr. Ambedkar.

(vii) Studied Buddhism; the principles of Buddhism taught me way and truth.

(vii) I was 10 at the time of 1956 conversion. At a later stage I realised I am no more a Hindu and untouchable.

(ix) Converted along with my parents in 1956.

(x) 'Reading books written by Ambedkar and his speeches—inspired to follow Dr. Ambedkar's thoughts'.

To the question whether change of religion is spiritually satisfying—all had replied 'yes' and some have substantiated why.

To the question whether the purpose for which converted has been achieved, the answers, asserted, were:

1. Created new outlook towards life; All superstitions decayed (ended); achieved much of what Dr. Ambedkar wanted us to achieve; principle of Buddhism helps in daily life; achieved the goal of self-respect; freed from the bondage of rituals; raised status;

2. One said: "spiritually, I could get nothing. But politically and socially, I have achieved everything".

3. Three responded that the purpose have not been *fully* achieved.

The answers to the questions confirm the impact that Neo-Buddhism has made on the ex-Mahars. We can conclude safely that the change of religion has made a deep impact on the Neo-Buddhists socially and religiously.

It was pointed out in this study that the conversion into Buddhism by the Mahars was not on the basis of spiritual quest, i.e., by conviction that Buddhism is more spiritually satisfying. Even Dr. Ambedkar first was on the lookout for a suitable alternate to Hinduism and it was in this process that he found the uniqueness of Buddhism over other religions which he considered. Then he guided his fellow Mahars on the greatness of Buddhism as he had been guiding them in sociological and political matters. As noted earlier, Dr. Ambedkar must have taken the clue by the 'Mass Movement' of Christian conversions in which, while converting the downtrodden and depressed classes, the Christian missionaries, as pointed out earlier, adopted the policy of 'convert first; catechise later'. This exactly has happened. It may be said to the credit of Dr. Ambedkar that one single man, who was not a Buddhist missionary or monk, nor he conducted catechism classes for the prospective converts, nor he conducted 'evangelistic campaigns' on the social gospel of the Buddha nor did he gratify them, effected such a mass conversion pro-Buddhism while a multitude of Christian missionaries who ministered in India struggled to achieve conversions; or which the conquering Mughals did achieve by their swords and lances. On the basis of the survey conducted by the author, we have recorded compliment that Buddhism gives not only spiritual satisfaction but gives a zest for life.

We may assert that direct impact among the downtrodden mass on the whole—at national leval—is evident in the emergence of the Dalit Society, focussing the problems of the Depressed Classes to the Indian Society at large. *Dalit Voice* is their official organ. Now the *Dalit Voice* indicates the magnetic attraction of the *Dalits* towards Buddhism. We may cite the following reporting as an example:

> "S. Swatantra Rao, a Telugu *Dalit* IAS Officer of the Karnataka cadre, received the coveted International award of `Bhim Ratna' in the historic Grand Committee Room of the House of Commons, London on April 14 (1992)... Mr. Rao was told by the Dalits living in U.K. that they were angry with the `educated' Dalits living in India. The Indian Dalit leadership is betraying Babasahib by not embracing Buddhism. Despite reservations extended to Buddhists, the educated Dalits are sticking to the world's most uncivilised religion, they said. Mr. Rao assured that he would soon embrace Buddhism".[3]

The impact of Neo-Buddhism, which sparked off in 1956 at Nagpur among a particular community spread over in Maharashtra. It has now grown to be a nationwide 'event' of the *Dalits*. This is why we find that the numerical strength of the Buddhists is growing fast at the national level.

ON THE INDIAN SOCIETY

The second impact of Neo-Buddhism, now getting wide spread all over India is not only in the bringing in of all *Dalits* together, but also in serving the country by making available talented and capable people to assume greater responsibilities, like the IAS, IPS, management positions in industries, business houses and padagogy—leave alone professional careers like doctors, engineers and lawyers, etc.

Negatively, even today, those who are caste-conscious are not able to realise the reality of the *Dalits* coming up. Superiority complex, specially among the higher castes of non-Brahmins, seems to be deep-rooted against the untouchables all over India. Dr. Borale's analysis of this element seems to be tenable. He says: "Socio-economic segregation is still in existence in India. What is the main reason of all sorts of segregation? According to *Vishnu Smriti*, the choosing of the name of Sudra must indicate `contempt', unlike the `Dwija classes', namely—`auspicious' in the case of Brahmana, `power' in the case of Kshatriya, and `wealth' in the case of Vaishya. `Contempt', therefore, is the basis of segregation".[4] By this, we may understand that, because of `contempt' from within, the higher caste tend to keep the *Dalits* under subjection who seem to progress economically and socially. As Dr. Borale says further, "Dias and Hughes, while defining law, state that law is an instrument used by the economically ruling class to keep the subordinate class in subjection"[5]. Caste system would continue to be a hindrance, so it seems, "against all wishful thinking, it has not gone out. Though it appears to be getting out, really speaking, we can say it has only loosened its tight belt. When we talk about red-tapism in Government offices seldom would we realise the woes the low caste people have to suffer." To quote Prof. Pande: "There is some truth in saying that some officers are inclined towards the ill-feelings of caste, religions, etc. which hinders the meeting of desired goals".[6] For some, worshipping in a temple is an unbearable experience, when the temple is financed by an untouchable community. (This fact is evidenced by the fatal assault on the Lingayats *Dalits* in March 1993 in Karnataka, just because the untouchables gained entry into the temple, where Lingayats were worshipping, though the *Dalits* had pooled Rs. 10,000 for the renovation of that temple.) In such a situation can we say that, caste system is on its way out? Prof. Pande is correct in saying that "the Schedule Castes as a social group, still continue to be the most lagging social class".[7]

In this context we must note that the Bharatiya Janata Party, which met at Calcutta recently, had adopted a new election strategy. *India Today* records: "As another element of its electoral strategy, the BJP will be promoting

Swami Vivekananda, B.R. Ambedkar, and Mahatma Gandhi as its heroes. Gandhi's conception of Ram Rajya will be weaved into the party's determination to construct the temple at Ayodhya. 'Hindu awakening, Ram Rajya and social equality' will be the slogans of the BJP in the next election".[8] It is surprising to note that the BJP is willing to project the 'social equality' concept of an Indian, who called Hindu religion as a 'visitation' and not only denounced it, but renounced it as well!

By embracing Neo-Buddhism the downtrodden *Dalits* did and do reduce the sociological problems of India considerably, though it tends to lead to law and order problems, sometimes.

As we try to analyse the numerical strength of the Buddhists in India we get ambiguous and incongruous figures. Needless to mention that, before the invasions of the Mughals in India, there were Buddhists all over the country, despite dispersion during persecution by the anti-Buddhist kingdoms and empires. Subsequently, after the establishment of the British Indian Empire and its consolidation, the Indian Empire extended from Baluchistan in the West, Burma (Myanmar) and other far Eastern countries in the East and Ceylon (Sri Lanka) in the South. This author has examined the Census figures from 1881 and whenever we read of religious populace in the British Empire, it includes such a vast territory including many Indian princely States and some Asia Pacific countries and now when we say India, it is hardly half of what it used to be till 1921. We read in the Census of 1921: "Buddhism is the most dominant religion of the indigenous races of Burma and some of the tribes of Eastern Himalayas and tracts of Kashmir which border on Tibet. It is the official religion of the small State of Sikkim. The proportion of Buddhists per 1000 persons of the Indian Empire has increased with the steady rise in the population of Burma itself due to the increasing immigration of Indians is 15, 50,000 in 1881 to

276,000 in 1921".[9] We further note that 85 per cent of the entire Buddhist population of the British Indian Empire was of Burma and other Far East Asian countries: when they became independent, remained predominantly Buddhist and so it seems that the Buddhist population in Indian has been reducing. But what really had happened in India was obliteration of Buddhism long ago.

When Anagarika Dhammapala left for England at the turn of the century in Madras Presidency alone there were 12,000 Buddhists. Then other places where Buddhism was revived, what should have been the Buddhist population as the 20th century was dawning? Within a period of five years (1956-61) the population of Buddhists registered a spectacular increase of 1670 per cent (i.e. from 1,80,823 it rose to 32,50, 227.)[10] Almost the same percentage of increase is furnished by Mahasthawir Sangharakshita in his *Ambedkar and Buddhism* (1671 per cent). But, taking one decimal point it ought to be 1697.5 per cent, i.e., almost 1700 per cent of increase of Buddhist population between 1951 and 1961, more precisely between 1956 and 1961. However, *The Statesman*, one of India's leading dailies, interpreted the Census of 1961, in which it was reported that for every Buddhist in 1951, there were 1671 others in 1961.[11] This minor mistake apart, what is important is to note its phenomenal growth. According to 1971 Census the Buddhist population was 38,12,325. According to 1981 it was reported to be 47,19,796. Therefore, we may interpolate that if any substantial numerical strength of Buddhists is registered in the census of India, it could be deemed due to Neo-Buddhist movement. We must also note that the majority of this Buddhist community is from Maharashtra. Traditional Buddhists being more or less the same and insignificant, the phenomenal growth is the contribution of the Neo-Buddhist sect. Further, Buddhist refugees from Tibet are not reflected in this census, who are spread all over the country, either as nomadic businessmen selling wool-wear or those encamped in settlements.

IMPACT OVERSEAS

We find a definite impact of Neo-Buddhism in the United Kingdom. We note through *Ambedkar Lehar* that there was a demonstration against atrocities committed by the caste Hindus against untouchables in London on 17th September 1978. This evidences that a lot of the untouchables have migrated to England, where the caste discrimination is meted out, not with the sanction of the British Government but as two 'unadjustable' British Indian communities creating social problems in the United Kingdom. We find that most of the Dalits there have embraced Buddhism, and as we had noted a while ago, the Dalits there are taking the issue of conversion into Buddhism as a tribute to Dr. Ambedkar. Earlier we had noted that a Dalit IAS Officer was asked by the Neo-Buddhists in London to embrace Buddhism. We must also not forget that Mahasthavir Sangharakshita, the British monk, is now residing in the UK and he is the one who was close to Dr. Ambedkar and imparted Buddhist castechism a little before and a while after the demise of Dr. Ambedkar, we also learn that 'Bhimratna' award is instituted by the Dalits in the UK. There are a few Buddhists living in Canada and in Sri Lanka, deeply interested in the ideologies of Dr. Ambedkar.

There are at least two known American scholars who are interested in the post-Ambedkar movement. The name of Dr. Eleanor Zelliot of the Carlton College, Minnesota, USA is known in the Neo-Buddhist circles and has been a great source of inspiration to many Neo-Buddhists of India. A quote from Dr. Zelliot: "It is rare when a man's influence not only lasts but increases after his death, but this is certainly the case of Dr. B.R. (Babasaheb) Ambedkar. The movement toward politics, religions, social and economic equality which he dominated from 1920 until his death in 1956 still continues. That movement also finds new rays, in such areas as literature, drama, art and women's activities. Since Babasaheb is still an inspiration, an innovator and a challenger, every detail of his life retains importance for societies which are committed to human advancement. His life-history offers lesson for all of us and it offers hope as well".[12]

Among the American scholars who are evincing keen interest in Neo-Buddhism, the name of Dr. Christopher Queen of Harvard University, USA is bound to be heard louder in the days to come. He came to India to visit Buddhist pockets, but was exposed to Dr. Ambedkar's involvement in the revival of Buddhism in India and now he, as a "Christian-Buddhist"*, is a fast growing Religion Movement in the USA is taking keen interest in Dr. Ambedkar's movement. He says in an article: "As American Buddhism searches for authentic models of social and political action, the figure of Dr. B.R. Ambedkar deserves to be better known. Following a tumultuous career as a leader of India's untouchables and architect of India's Constitution. Ambedkar converted to Buddhism in his final years and formulated a socially engaged Buddhism which addresses contemporary issue of economic justice, social identity and political freedom".[13] (When the author met him at Harvard University, Boston, USA in August 1992, he was greeted by Dr. Queen with *Jai Bheem.!*)

The study of the impact of Dr. Ambedkar and Neo-Buddhism overseas would constitute a research by itself. To note that a non-Philosopher (in the traditional understanding of the word 'Philosopher'), who was known in India as a champion of the downtrodden and depressed classes and the chief architect of India's Constitution was

---

* 'Christian Buddhist' is a fast growing religious movement in the USA.

also well known in the Far Eastern and other Buddhist countries as the reviver of Buddhism in India is a matter of pride for any Indian.

Though his *Buddha and His Dhamma* was shocking to these traditional Buddhist countries, Dr. Ambedkar was acknowledged as a genuine Buddhist (even before his conversion) in those countries. To excite and inspire scholars overseas is indeed incredible.

The movement started off by Dr. B.R. Ambedkar for the downtrodden people in India, may become universal one day—echoing the socio-religious philosophy of Dr. Ambedkar with reverberations. On the 14th April 1993 at Jersey city in the USA, a bronze statue of Dr. Ambedkar was unveiled.[14]

REFERENCES

1. Sastri, Sankaranand, *Ambedkar on Buddhist Conversion and its Impact,* (ed.,) Eastern Book Linkers, Delhi, 1990, p. 19.
2. *Ibid.,* p. 9.
3. *Dalit Voice,* Vol. II, June 1-15, No. 14, 1992, p. 6.
4. Dongre, M.K., *The Economic Thoughts of Dr. Ambedkar,* (Dr. P.T. Borale's foreword), p. xiii.
5. *Ibid.,* p. xiv.
6. Pande, G.C. & Pande, P.C., *Social Anatomy of Economic Growth,* p. 530.
7. *Ibid.,* p. 538.
8. *India Today,* April 30, 1993, p. 55.
9. *Census of India,* 1921, p. 115.
10. Cf. Ahir, D.C., *Buddhism in Modern India,* p. 38.

11. Presler, Dr. H.H., 'Neo-Buddhist Stir in India', *India Cultures Quarterly*, Jabalpur, 1964, p. 2.
12. Cf. Kadam, K.N. (Ed) *Dr. Babasaheb Ambedkar and the Significance of His Movement*, p. vii.
13. Queen, Dr. Christopher, (Research article) *Re-inventing the Wheel—Dr. Ambedkar and the Politics of Compassion*, p. 1.
14. Cf. *Rani Muthu*,(Tamil Edition), No. 292, Madras, April, 1993, p. 3.

9

CONCLUSION

Dr. B.R. AMBEDKAR—A CRITIQUE

1. Ambedkar—The Man

We usually eulogies people after their demise, whether we mean it or not. But when one eulogises Ambedkar, it seems that the word `eulogy' itself is eulogised and honoured.

Nothing can perhaps be more valid than the tributes of critics. The opinion of Shri C. Rajagopalachari, a strong protagonist of the Chaturvarnya System, said of Ambedkar: "Ambedkar was a thoroughly upright person and a man with a keen jurist sense, a proud and irreconcilable heart, great learning and when approached in right spirit, full of friendliness".[1]

It may be appropriate to quote the tribute of *The New York Times,* (USA): "Ambedkar was known and honoured throughout the world chiefly as a champion of the untouchables. What is perhaps not so well-known is that he put a profound impress upon India's major legal structures".[2] Dr. Rajendra Prasad's tribute concerns Ambedkar's political and sociological contribution. He said: "Ambedkar was the architect of our Constitution and his services in various capacities, particularly for the uplift of the Depressed Classes, cannot be exaggerated".[3] The general nature of Ambedkar was one of total sincerity. He insisted on moral character and maintained it himself. Even the reason why he married for the second time, long after he became a widower, was on moral grounds. He is reported to have written in a letter: "... My friends tell me that if I am not ready to marry, then I must seek some nurse to look after me and also to keep the house. I have been thinking about it for a long time, but such a thing may lead to doubts in minds of the people. Therefore, marriage appears a better way. I had made a vow not to marry after the death of Yeshwanta's mother. But the circumstances are forcing me to break this vow. Doctors clearly say that I have to prefer between marriage or early death".[4] Dr. Ambedkar did not limit his understanding of morality only in terms of physical character, but a morality *in toto,* in all spheres of his activities and obligations.

Hardwork was unique of Dr. Ambedkar. As a student in the USA and UK, he is said to have worked for eighteen hours a day. Even back home it is difficult to believe that he was actively involved in social and political movements, as a leader and yet he could find time to publish original research papers, articles, make thorough studies of Hinduism, Christianity, Islam, Sikhism and Buddhism, draft Constitution (almost single handedly) and write *Buddha and His Dhamma*. In between travels overseas and within India attending International Conferences or addressing public meetings he could balance his timings. Ambedkar's extraordinary academic accomplishments, his foreign education, sacrificing lucrative Government jobs for the sake of his community's welfare, stylish and impressive personality, soul-stirring speeches, unfailing devotion to the cause of the 'untouchables'—all these made him a 'charismatic hero' as Dr. Presler calls him in another context.[5]

2. Ambedkar, the Founder of Neo-Buddhism

We have seen how and why Ambedkar founded Neo-Buddhism. We have also emphasised that it was not on a religious satisfaction and bliss experienced in Buddhism that Ambedkar relinquish Hinduism. It was a `reverse causality'. Having decided to relinquish Hinduism, he looked for suitable alternate religions. In this too, as noted earlier, he was giving weightage not only to spiritualism, but also materialism and nationalism. Subsequently, he was attracted by the spiritual, social, political and scientific (rational) dimensions of Buddhism. Having decided on Buddhism he drew closer and closer to becoming a Buddhist. It appears that his procrastination to become a Buddhist by taking the vows might be due to the fact that he was not yet fully ready to accept Buddhism in its totality and his intense moral fervour might not have allowed him to accept openly a religion which he was not fully ready to be quickened by his conscience to make a public confession as his faith. Obviously it was not a question of an old flame of Hinduism lingering in him to take two long decades to accept another religion as his own.

The main reasons for his accepting Buddhism are undoubtedly the factors of human dignity and social justice. He tried social reforms and it appeared to him a struggle endless. His decision to embrace Buddhism was to realise human dignity, equality, liberty and justice in his own life. He told his people—the Mahars—of his decision and they followed him to the hilt.

We can easily infer that Ambedkar's idea of a Buddhist faith was a perfect religion as it is, it should have a compact and perfect system of 'Church' Administration.

A spiritual and 'evangelistic' clergy of monks (probably of either sexes) and a compact compendium of scriptures like the *Bible, Quran* or *Adigranth*. He did have a vision to open a Buddhist seminary to train the future Buddhist monks. Had he been alive he would have actualised this vision. His understanding of Buddhism was that of scientific religion, devoid of any supernatural elements in it. To make it relevant to the changed situation in India and the circumstances in which he and his fellow-Mahars were embracing Buddhism he introduced an additional set of twenty-two vows, mentioned earlier.

3. Ambedkar and the Buddha

Despite the time lag of more than two millenium years, there are many similarities between the *Sakyamuni* of yore and the statesman of our times. First of all, many have, amongst the Buddhists in India and abroad, begun to think of Ambedkar as another *Bodhisattva*. This idea, as far as Ambedkar is concerned, should be done away with rationally. However, hypothetically, we can accept the concept of *Bodhisattva* as one who works for the salvation of others as applicable to Dr. Ambedkar.

The background in the births of the Buddha and Dr. Ambedkar is, of course, radically different. Yet, early marriage is one resemblance between the two. But we must note that while the Buddha left home and strove to attain 'enlightenment'—he underwent strenuous self-imposed discipline and literally made his body, skin and bone. In the modern circumstances, we see Dr. Ambedkar leaving homeland in pursuit of knowledge working very hard. Like the Buddha after enlightenment who rebelled against the social structure of his times, Dr. Ambedkar, after his return from the USA, rebelled against the social structure of his own times. The Buddha was an itinerant preacher, so was Dr. Ambedkar. Both rediculed the scriptural authority of the Vedas. Both were concerned about the equality and welfare of women of their respective times.

Both, Buddha and Ambedkar, lived chaste lives and were above blame morally. They could set examples for others to emulate. But while the Buddha was exclusively interested in the spiritual welfare, sociological aspects beings incidéntal, Dr. Ambedkar worked in various capacities for the welfare of various sections of people keeping the national unity in mind. It was only after embracing Buddhism that his impact is felt in great dimensions.

Of the differences, the Buddha's approach to his opponents was persuasion throwing convincing arguments, whereas, Ambedkar's approach was by assertion, aggravated and marked by rash statements, with brash adjectives. It was pointed out by a critic that while the Buddha's Buddhism was based on love, Ambedkar's Neo-Buddhism was based on hatred. Human nature varies and incarnations too have varied proportions. So, we have to keep in our mind Ambedkar's background before arriving at conclusions about his self and his attitude to the society that was around him.

4. Final Analysis

Ambedkar was indeed a great man. We may even go to the extent of saying that after Mahatma Gandhi, if any 2Indian could stake his claim for international recognition as one of the greatmen of the world in modern times it could be only Ambedkar. He would easily be compared with Dr. Martin Luther King, Jr. in many respects. His contribution was not limited to the emancipation of the oppressed and downtrodden people of the Indian society, not only for the great role he played in the drafting and finalising the Constitution of India, but also his reviving as the deadwood in the history of religions of India—Buddhism, and giving it a new look as a sociological avenue and spiritual satisfaction for the downtrodden societies in India, of the Dalits. His occasional ill-temperament, hard-hitting and verulent adjectives, provocative speeches and explosive disposition against injustice may be deemed as those caused by the oppressive features of the Indian society and hence he may be exonerated.

Politically, the Bahujan Samaj Party of Indian politics is Ambedkar's posthumous legacy. This party is doing yeomen service to the cause of the Dalits, has come to be recognised as a powerful political party. Ambedkar's contribution in the field of sociology has been so much that scholars and sociological research organisations have plenty of material to draw clues from and develop into great sociological research forums. The study of Dr. Ambedkar's sociological theories may one day be reckoned as the first of its kind in India and it may lead to international research. Our relating the theories of Robert Baldwin, Max Weber and Emile Durkheim to Ambedkar's socio-religious thoughts leading to the reality of 'Neo-Buddhism' (something nostalgic and yet new) was to focus the international understanding of sociology, economics and philosophy of religion as a three-fold combine. Ambedkar's psyche had a great bearing leading to *'Neo-Buddhism'* and thus it may interest scholars of psychology of religion. There is a vast scope of research which Dr. Ambedkar offers through his thoughts and actions. 'Neo-Buddhism' itself offers scope for continued researches in the history of religions. Therefore, we may submit that Dr. Ambedkar is a lasting and inspiring name to generations of sociologists, historians of religions, economists and politicians.

In the history of modern India, Dr. Ambedkar's significant contribution to the various fields in India can be abridged to the Indian Constitution, social justice and, above all, revival of Buddhism. The importance of Dr. Ambedkar is now realised all over India through belatedly and posthumously. He has rightly been awarded the highest honour of India—the 'Bharat Ratna'. The recognition of his calibre at the international level is growing steadily and he may carve a niche for himself not only as an Indian celebrity but also as one of the world's greatmen of the twentieth century.

NEO-BUDDHISM—A CRITIQUE

'Neo-Buddhism' is mostly recognised in India as 'Buddhism' itself, in the conventional sense. For the general public, it is but difficult to imagine that Mahayana, Hinayana and the lesser known Neo-Buddhism are all one. Even after three centuries of Christianity existing in India, how many non-Christians would know that differences exist between two major sects of Christianity, namely, Protestantism and Roman Catholicism? or even after seven centuries of Muslim presence in India, how many would know the distinguishing features of Shias and Sunnis? These two great religions of the world, as far as Indians are concerned, are alien religions but have taken deep roots in India. Unfortunately, one wonders if it would be an exaggeration to say that Buddhism, now in India, is enjoying only the 'alien' understanding, despite the fact that the Buddha was born in India, and preached first in India. There are many great places of Buddhist importance in the country but where is Buddhism as a way of life? The seriousness of Ambedkar and his fellow Mahars in embracing Buddhism, or for that matter, the seriousness of millions of Mahars snapping ties with Hinduism appears not to have been of considerable significance for most of the Indians. It caused only a flutter. Its seriousness and consequence is getting gradually known and realised; first it was realised in Maharashtra and then in other parts of India.

1. The Problem of Pre-Fix 'Neo'

The question did arise as to what kind of Buddhists Ambedkar and his fellow Mahars would be, sectwise. Ambedkar had said at the Press Conference on 13th October 1956, that it would be neither Mahayana nor Hinayana, but would be 'Sort of Neo-Buddhism or

Navayana'. Therefore, the word 'Neo-Buddhism' was coined by Ambedkar himself. What Ambedkar had replied spontaneously to the enquiring press came to be dubbed permanently.

'Neo' means, 'new', 'later', 'revived in modified form', and 'based upon'.[6] We can surmise that Ambedkar must have positively borne in mind the meaning—'revived in modified form'. Ambedkar was adroit at the correct usage of English words and the word 'Neo' came to stay to cause unnecessary misunderstanding to imply 'New' and not connote what it was intended to imply 'revived in modern form'. There are many Neo-Buddhists who do not appreciate the usage of the prefix 'Neo'. To quote two positive opinions, in the questionnaire distributed by this author against the question, 'Any other point you would like to mention', the following two opinions emerged:

1. "I would like to bring to your notice that the topic of your study is wrong. You have termed it as 'Neo-Buddhism' which is absolutely wrong. We have embraced Buddhism preached by the Lord Buddha for the welfare of mankind under the able leadership of Dr. Babasaheb Ambedkar. Our conversion was really unique. Therefore, our critics started calling us 'Neo-Buddhist' which is not acceptable to us. Hundreds of people have embraced Christianity or Islam, but they are not called Neo-Christian or Neo-Muslim. Why so?"

2. "According to my strong opinion, this should not have been mentioned in this questionnaire, as a Neo-Buddhist questionnaire. Because, by naming Neo-Buddhist, you are keeping them (as) separate group who are converted (to) Buddhism, ultimately treated again a particular class or caste, as were discarded by Hindus as untouchables."

The major flaw with this prefix is that it indicates that any 'Neo-Buddhist' is an 'ex-untouchable Hindu' and as such is abominable as it mars the very purpose of conversion. The bitter memories linger on by this prefix. What Dr. Ambedkar uttered in an interview to connote a different meaning altogether, the undesirable alternate implication of English has stuck on. In Christianity if there is no difference between the 'Jew' or 'Gentile', so also in Indian Buddhism there cannot be any difference between 'ex-Brahman' or 'ex-Barbarian'. A Buddhist has to be taken as a Buddhist, without any string attached to his past. The ambiguity will cease only when the prefix 'Neo' is eliminated or understood in its correct perspective. The word 'Neo-Buddhist' more than giving a new identity to the ex-untouchable, retains indirectly the old identity of the ex-untouchable Buddhist. The caste continues to haunt as a ghost in the life of a Neo-Buddhist. Hence the term 'Neo-Buddhism' is detrimental not only to the interests of the new convert, but to Indian Buddhism revived by Dr. Ambedkar on the whole. However, until the prefix 'Neo' is dropped consciously and universally, Ambedkar-sponsored Buddhism will be known as 'Neo-Buddhism' only.

Neo-Buddhism can be understood and should be done so, as the Buddhism revived in modern form by Ambedkar with emphasis on both scientific and rational approach, as a religion bearing the concepts of liberty, equality and fraternity as the very foundations of its belief and proffering social, economic and intellectual development in an individual.

2. The Problem of Structure

No religion is complete without the following basic organisational structure, namely, (a) The Founder, (b) The Clergy—the priestly class, (c) Scripture/Scriptures, and (d) The Laymen. Though the laymen are the very strength of any religious movement, in an organised religious structure, they form the fourth order of dynamics. However dynamic the laity may be, without a properly organised priestly class, they would be left for themselves and in most cases they would be like 'a ship without a captain'. The clergy are very important to understand and interpret the scriptures, to counsel those in need, to catechise and to evangelise. The absence of the clergy is conspicuous in Neo-Buddhism.

The problem seems to begin with the question who the founder of Neo-Buddhism is. If Neo-Buddhism is taken as a sect of Buddhism, and it ought to be taken so, then the Buddha is the very founder of (Neo) Buddhism and 'Neo'-Buddhism is a *Navayana* form of Buddhism. But, Dr. Ambedkar, being in the hearts and minds of each and everyone of the Mahars and other Dalits, his place is pre-eminent and hence Neo-Buddhism is made to appear as an off-shoot of 'Lord Buddha and Dr. Ambedkar' combine. In comparison Dr. Ambedkar could be considered as what Swami Vivekananda was to Sri Ramakrishna Paramahamsa. In fact, Dr. Ambedkar was like Prophet Mohammed in Islam, or like the tenth Guru in Sikhism. In terms of Buddhism, Dr. Ambedkar could be deemed to have founded the *Navayana* form of Buddhism as was Nagarjuna founding the *Mahayana*. A convert in the first batch of converts, Shri Shinde, told the author few years ago that Bhagwan Buddha and Babasaheb Ambedkar are like his two eyes.

In a rational religion like Neo-Buddhism, identification of the founder poses certain problems. When a man, who is known and identified as the emancipator, liberator and saviour—a *marga-data* by the mass and when that *marga-data* points to another man as the *marga-data*, both of them have equal importance for the mass. Butt Dr. Ambedkar who has been seen, known, heard and lived with as one among them has left such a deep impression in the hearts and minds of his followers. The veneration given to that 'man' is shared with yet another venerable one whom they have not seen, known and heard. Is it an identity crisis, to relate the present continuous to past continuous? One of the respondents to the questionnaire of this author, when asked

"What does Dr. Ambedkar mean to you"? stated: "Not a point to mean less than the 'Lord'". Another responded: 'Lord'. Another responded: "He was a reformer, but now gradually taking the place of Lords". Yet another said: "For me, Dr. Ambedkar is a *marga-data* (path giver) and *marga-deshak* (path shower)". One responded: "I respect Dr. Ambedkar as a Bodhisattva". Under the circumstances, it will take many generations of the Buddhists of Dalit origin to understand and differentiate the significances of the Buddha and Dr. Ambedkar in their proper perspectives. To enable them to differentiate thus, Buddhist clergy is badly needed to work among the (Neo) Buddhists of the present day Indian society and educate them.

3. Problem of Interpretation

One of the greatest services that Dr. Ambedkar had done to Indian Buddhism, as noted earlier, is to compile the important features of Buddhist empiricism, codify them and present in a single compendium—*Buddha and His Dhamma*. This is the Scriptures of the 'Neo' or *Navayana* Buddhist faith, which has all that Dr. Ambedkar wanted to say, the *Buddha and His Dhamma*, says Sangharakshita, "can, in fact, be compared to a well planned, solidly built and beautifully decorated palace, some apartments of which the architect was obliged to leave unfinished. Though they are unfinished, so splendid is the palace as a whole and so perfectly inhabitable, that as one enters the lofty portals and starts looking around, one is struck less by any incompleteness in the execution of the work as by the genius of the architect and the grandeur of his overall design".[7] This, in nutshell, is the content of the book usually said to be the *magnum opus* of Dr. Ambedkar, as an emphathetic critic viewed it.

While Mahasthavir Sangharakshita sees the *Buddha and His Dhamma* as a magnificent palace, though somewhat incomplete, there are many reviewers who found the work totally 'wanting'.

Dr. Presler cites and holds that "some of the sources of Ambedkar conception of Buddhism may be outside the Buddhist canon".[8]

To answer this criticism of Dr. Presler, we may state that it is not important if the words of secular literature and phraseologies are borrowed to drive home effectively certain points. It is important that such 'borrowings' do not dilute the relevance of the message and convey in contemporary language. We note this trend in St. Paul's epistles to convey the Christian messages borrowing the secular traditions prevailing at that time.

Another criticism Dr. Presler advances is that the *Buddha and His Dhamma* does not contain footnotes or other references or list of sources, which is inappropriate to a writer holding a Ph.D. from Columbia University and a D.Sc. from London School of Economics.

To answer this criticism, we can only say that Dr. Ambedkar did not have time to prepare a list of references as he was dead even before print was complete.

Another criticism of Dr. Presler is about Ambedkar's method of discerning between what the Buddha said and what in his own opinion Buddha could not have said. Dr. Presler concludes that "the basic scriptures of Neo-Buddhism, are partly 'Neo' and partly 'Buddhist', as 'possibly Ambedkar's tests of authenticity would not satisfy a historian's science of documents; they leave the door open for subjectivism and prejudices".

Another criticism of Dr. Presler is about Ambedkar's rejection of traditional teachings of Hinayana which to Ambedkar is absurd. The four problems of life, according to Dr. Presler, "arose in Ambedkar's mind because of his world-affirming, life-affirming, social philosophy clashed with the world-negating, life-denying ideology of Hinayana Buddhism. Ambedkar believed life to be an egg; Buddha believed it to be a bubble. Perhaps his social philosophy was Ambedkar's norm, and possibly he bent Buddha's norm around it".[9] (p. 18)

We must note here that the basic difference between classical Buddhism and Neo-Buddhism is that while the former is world-negating, the latter is world-affirming. Ambedkar interpreted Buddhism to the oppressed section of the Indian society, not like Christianity that the 'reward' was in the world to come. Here the reward is to be attained in this very world. So, Buddhism, as interpreted by him is world-affirming. Even if Ambedkar had bent 'The Buddha's teachings' to his thinking, his explanation would have been what he told once; that there is flexibility inherent in Buddhism not seen in any other religion.

We may mention here that the absence of Neo-Buddhist clergy is conspicuous for an important reason. The live-wire of any religion is its festivities. Who are to be at the fore-front? Who should be at any home at births, betrothals, wedding and funerals? Where are the clergy in Neo-Buddhism for all these?

4. The Problem of the Sangha

In the Buddhist set-up, even from the time of the Buddha, *Sangham* was one of the important features. It is an act of taking refuge in *Sangham* as much as in *Buddham* and *Dhammam*. One of the reasons for the extinction of Buddhism in India was the deprivity of the Buddhist monks, morally, intellectually and spiritually. After the revival efforts of Anagarika Dhammapala from the turn of the century, Buddhist monks from Sri Lanka and other Buddhist countries had been visiting India, reviving Buddhism and renovating vihars. The Mahabodhi Society, however, was managed by caste Hindus, with Buddhist monks under them. Ambedkar was disappointed with this lacuna and this led him to observe that the Buddhist Bhikkus were not doing what the Buddha had expected of a Bhikku. Therefore, the *Sangha* had become meaningless to him, at least in the Indian context. Hence, he did not want to take the vow on *Sangha*, when he got converted to Buddhism. He wanted the Bhikkus in India to be as the Buddha had intended them to be: "What was the object of the Buddha in creating the Bhikku? ...to create a perfect man or to create a social servant devoting his life to the service of the people? If the Bhikku is only a perfect man, he is of no use to the propagation of Buddhism, because though perfect, he is selfish. If, on the other hand, he is a social servant, he may prove to be the hope of Buddhism"[9]. Ambedkar's vision of a *Bhikku* is of one who would propagate Buddhism by social actions. This would imply mixing with people, listening to their woes, participating in their struggles, sharing their joys and sorrows and so on.

The *Sangha* in India had two kinds of monks, those of the *Mahayana* sect and those from the *Hinayana*. This author has met and interviewed two monks in Nagpur, one from Sri Lanka who was an upholder of the *Hinayana* form—(Bhikku Gunaratne) and another from Japan, a Mahayana Buddhist (Reverend Sure Sasayee). With these divergent and clashing teachings, what would become of an illiterate Neo-Buddhist? Ambedkar tried to present a simple path. But his sudden demise literally orphanated the Neo-Buddhists. The *Buddha and His Dhamma* was published in English. Ambedkar had presented the teachings in simple English unusual of his practice. This facilitated even the less educated lot. Subsequently, this was translated into Hindi to make it available for many. But to explain the insights therein and to answer critics, there isn't any Buddhist monk in the order even today. Dr. Ambedkar as noted earlier, had planned to start a Buddhist seminary to recruit and train Buddhist monks in India. This is an unfulfilled dream of Dr. Ambedkar. Therefore, the Neo-Buddhists need to organise themselves to establish amongst them the priestly class as per the guidelines which their mentor, Dr. Ambedkar, provided. There is a group of Neo-

Buddhist elite which could not accept the *Bodhisatva* status of Dr. Ambedkar. There are some who would not hesitate to incorporate in their personal beliefs the Four Noble Truths which Ambedkar had rejected. Yet, in form and substance, they believe in the other Buddhist doctrines which Ambedkar stipulated in his *magnum opus*. Before the dogmatic differences could crop up, there must be established doctrines, unique for the *Navayana* form of Indian Buddhism.

It may be observed that at *Diksha Bhoomi* (Nagpur): Ambedkar's statue is venerated as a ritual on his birth anniversary (14th April) and the great conversion day (14th October). Some fall prostrate, some break coconuts, some offer *agarbathis*—certainly *not* as superstition, but as a mark of devotion and veneration. The irony is that the Vihara which is adjacent is bypassed by many!

The strength of Neo-Buddhism is its rational approach. To make it seems as such in a challenging secular environment of India, Neo-Buddhism, first of all, should shed the word 'Neo' and make it Indian Buddhism of the *Navayana* form and rid of its shortcomings and synchratistic tendencies by an organised class of the clergy—the Buddhist monks and nuns.

NEO-BUDDHISTS—A CRITIQUE

We had already seen that Neo-Buddhism is a layman-oriented religion. Probably Ambedkar did not give much importance to having monks at the very inception of Neo-Buddhism as he had in mind thoroughly trained Bhikkus and Bhikkunis through a Buddhist seminary before launching them into Buddhist ministry. Shortly after conversion, he visited Kathmandu and his immediate project was to bring out the *Buddha and His Dhamma* which ought to have been published at the time of conversion ceremony itself. It was delayed and it was not printed until one year of his demise. He is said to have been working on the proofs till the very end of his life. Had he only lived a while longer, Neo-Buddhism, perhaps, would have had a perfect organisational set-up and an organised structure. That was not to be. It was only his inspiration that became the prime mover of the Neo-Buddhists since his *mahapari nibbana*. Every Neo-Buddhist is to propagate the *Dhamma*. Ambedkar even added that one-twentieth of the income of every Neo- Buddhist must be contributed for the propagation of the *Dhamma*, for he did not want any monetary help from any foreign country. He set moral standards for the Mahars and made them to take the vows while being initiated into Buddhism. He included a vow that Neo-Buddhists would do nothing which is detrimental to Buddhism.

We find that the Neo-Buddhists of today are following these precepts in letter and spirit meticulously. Ambedkar was once told that untouchables will remain untouchables no matter what he does to emancipate them. How wrong the critics have been was proved by Ambedkar! Except some cases these ex-untouchables of Neo-Buddhism are becoming a socially forward group. The mobility of the Neo-Buddhism is becoming an undeniable credibility. For all this, the unswerving loyalty of the second generation of the first batch of converts cannot be exaggerated.

The first three things a Neo-Buddhist demands are self-respect, human dignity and social equality. In the initial stages, scholarships and other facilities were denied to them, but subsequently the Government of Maharashtra resumed the economic benefits to the Mahars who became Buddhists. The present day second generation has taken full advantage of the same and has become highly qualified. It availed the reservation facilities and got into good jobs. Now, very seldom we see undereducated Neo-Buddhists. Self-confidence and boldness are manifest in them. They cannot tolerate injustice.

These being the general dispositions of the Neo-Buddhists, their standards of living are proportionate to their income. Many housewives of the Neo-Buddhists are educated; some of them are post-graduates. In a few families couples work in different offices. The inferiority complex which marks the personality of an individual belonging to the Scheduled Caste community, is missing in them, even among the women. Thus Ambedkar had fully succeeded in instilling the spirit of dignity and sense of equality.

The marriage process is endogamy. Cases of exagamy are found to be very rare; in such cases, often a Neo-Buddhist male finds his bride who happens to be a higher caste girl and is employed. That too, probably a colleague! in the homes of Neo-Buddhist faith, children are well taken care of. Some of them have great flair for language and literature. Whatever may be their language, they love writing on Dr. Ambedkar. The latest of a Dalit poet's genius in Sanskrit goes like this: *Buddha dharmo maha dharmo, Bharata bhatu sarvada, sarve paddalita loke prapna vantu samanatam* (Buddhism is a great religion; let it shine in Bharat. Let all downtrodden people in the universe attain equality).[10]

A deep Buddhist consciousness, aroused by Ambedkar, is now being voiced aloud and it is being heard. Every Neo-Buddhist house has the picture of Lord Buddha and of Dr. Ambedkar without fail. Equally true is that every educated man's house has a small or vast library containing Ambedkar's original writings, depending on the financial ability. In some cases a regular amount of income goes towards purchase of such books. Career-wise, while most of them feel secure in the vocations of their choice, some are ambitious. Intellectual type of Neo-Buddhists invariably take to Padagogy as their career, but some intellectuals, officers in Government or Banking services, spare time to find outlets for their intellectual tasks and stimulations. Some of them take to politics. Most of them, whatever their vocation, meet often to either discuss propagation of Buddhism and related matters.

Thus the Neo-Buddhists are, in fact, surpassing even those who come under the Backward Classes codification. A day might come when the present Neo-Buddhists, who by then would be reckoned as Indian Buddhists (*Navayana*), would be one among the forward communities of our country.

The most distinguishing form of greetings that the Neo-Buddhists have is to greet one another saying *Jai Bhim*. This unique way of greeting constantly reminds of their common bond of affinity. Watched closely one would see the warmth and affection one has for another.

A problem that is prevalent amongst the Neo-Buddhists—specially among businessmen and women—is the problem of syncreticism. This tendency of syncraticism eventually was one of the causes for Hinduism to devour Buddhism. Buddhism was forced out of India. If we would go to a market place in Nagpur and go to a prospering Neo-Buddhist businessman's shop, we would see invariably Lord Buddha's picture-photo on one end, Dr. Ambedkar's photo on the other end, and in between we may see Hindu Goddess Lakshmi's picture or idol. So also, the Hindu elements of fasts, use of *sindoor*, etc., are observed by some of the Neo-Buddhist women, or better termed wives of Neo-Buddhist men. In such cases, Indian culture is synonymous with Hindu culture and hence the uniqueness of the Neo-Buddhist identity is stained and corroded.

The case studies (please see annexures) are indicative of the benefits the ex-untouchables had derived by virtue of embracing Buddhism and their joy and delight rendering something in turn for the propagation of the *Dhamma*. It is not that the recipients of social benefits, by becoming Buddhists, stop after offering some subscription. We note that they offer in both cash and kind; someone spares two hours a day, someone writes, someone preaches and prays, and all contribute. This cheerful giving is unique. The respondents to the questionnaire were honest in their acknowledgement of the receipt of benefits because of embracing Buddhism.

As we have pointed out earlier, the Neo-Buddhists have been deprived of a specific leader. Yet they constitute an amalgamation of co-ordinated leadership from amongst themselves. There is no confusion, there is no internal bickerings. Each constituent is contributing his little mite and thus makes the effect enormous. The spirit of Ambedkar is in each of them and it is now catching up with the other parts of India today. The continued stream of mass conversions at different places, and at unsteady intervals are taking place.

The Indian Buddhists of *Navayana* tradition (Neo-Buddhists) however, cannot underestimate the importance of the priestly class—the monks and the nuns. The vision of Dr. Ambedkar has to be realised. The efficiency with which they are propagating the *Dhamma*, should be furthered to recruit and foster this vital factor in any religious movement. Until this is done, the efforts of Dr. Ambedkar to bring about a social change among the Mahars and other Depressed Classes through the path of the *Dhamma*, will remain incomplete. It has got to be done precisely as Ambedkar had visualised it.

To conclude, the study has been meaningful to this author as he looked around the various aspects of Neo-Buddhism *vis-a-vis* classical Buddhism. The *Dhammapada* of the Buddha has been the motivating factor of Dr. Ambedkar who, in his interpretation of Buddhism, brought out a radical change from all fronts of an untouchable—socio-religious and this continues to be an on-going dynamics.

We have seen that 'Neo'-Buddhism which this author would prefer to re-christen in its actual perspective as modern Indian Buddhism (*Navayana*) is a growing, powerful religious movement in India and it has sparked off international impact, an awareness of its meaningful existence in India.

Now Indian Buddhism with the *Navayana* sect needs a wider audience and has got to be re-recognised at the international level as a dynamic socio-religious sect in India. It will, in the near future.

REFERENCES

1. *Baba Saheb Ambedkar,* Amar Chitrakatha, Bombay, 1979, p. 32.
2. *Ibid.,* p. 32.
3. *Ibid.,* p. 32.
4. Bharathi K.S., *op. cit.,* p. 38.
5. Presler, Dr. H.H., *India Cultures Quarterly,* 1964, p. 23.
6. Collins *English Dictionary,* 1988 Ed.
7. Sangharakshita, *Ambedkar and Buddhism,* pp. 150-51.
8. Presler, Dr. H.H., *The Neo-Buddhist Stir in India,* pp. 15-22.
9. Ibid., p. 20.
10. Sanghasen Singh & Priya Sen Sing (ed.), *Ambedkar on Buddhist Conversion and its Impact,* p. 20.

ANNEXURE I NEO-BUDDHISM STUDY 1979

Questionnaire

1. Name ____________________
2. Age ____________________
3. Educational Qualifications ____________________
4. Caste ____________________
5. Profession ____________________
6. Address ____________________

   ____

   ____
7. Whether a Buddhist by birth or conversion ______
8. If a convert, reason why? ____________________

   ____

   ____

____

____

9. Has the purpose for which converted been achieved? If yes, how? __________________________

____

____

____

____

10. What does Dr. Ambedkar mean to you in your life? (Lord, Reformer, Incarnation, etc.)______________

____

11. If you belong to Scheduled Caste (like Mahar) or any other backward community, has your religion (Neo-Buddhism) given you any benefit (or advantage) in comparison with those belonging to higher castes?

____

____

____

____

12. Has your religion (Neo-Buddhism) helped you to gain any new status:

    (i) Financially ____________________________

    (ii) Socially_______________________________

13. Do you find your religion (Neo-Buddhism) spiritually satisfying. In what ways? ____________________

____

____

____

____

14. What is your opinion about: (i) Hinduism ______

______

______

______

(ii) Other religions ______

______

______

15. How much do you give (time and\or money) for the propagation of the Dhamma? ______

______

______

______

______

16. Any other point you may like to mention ______

______

______

______

______

Signature ______

Date ______

ANNEXURE II CONTRIBUTION OF NEO-BUDDHISTS

What is the contribution of Neo-Buddhists to the cause of Buddhism in India? This author's questionnaire, enclosed as an annexer, has sixteen questions in all. The *third* question was answered—out of fifteen select respondents, *eight* of them had left it blank or put in 'X' mark to emphasis no caste.

One responded: 'Before 1956, a Mahar and after, a Buddhist.

One responded: 'originally from Mahar'.

Two responded: 'Buddhist'.

Three responded: 'Mahar on records'. (They are in Government service.)

The responses to this question may be deemed as their conviction that by embracing Buddhism, there is no 'caste' at all. The old religion or caste is gone and is to be forgotten. Three who responded 'Mahar on Record', in answering other questions were Buddhists from within. To emphasise that they are Buddhists is a matter of pride and loosing the former caste, a privilege.

John F. Kennedy the late President of the USA, had said: "Ask not what your country has done for you, ask yourself what you have done for your country". If we adapt this quotation with a slight twist and ask a Neo-Buddhist.

A."What Buddhism has done for you", and

B."What you have done for Buddhism", the following answers would emerge. The first is that by embracing Buddhism, casteism is gone. If it is kept deliberately, it is only for records to avail benefits from the Government. The other aspects understanding of humanity.

1. A rickshaw puller, studied up to Pre Arts; Age 37, with fluency in both speaking and writing English: (He writes in English)

A.*Buddhism has given us full guidance of understanding and knowledge of humanity. There are only two castes, one is 'man' another is 'woman'.

B. *At my level best please (To the best of my ability).

(There are many undergraduates, who pull rickshaws or do other services, so as to give up their "ancestral profession" of the Mahars.)

2. *A medical representative, a graduate with a post-graduate diploma in management; Age 32.*

A. *As a Neo-Buddhist, I got all facilities which are awarded by the Indian Constitution to a Neo-Buddhist.

B. With my financial ability as much as possible, I devote and contribute to the cause of Buddhism.

3. *A Government employee, a graduate; Age 42.*

A. *Psychologically a Buddhist thinks himself equal to all, irrespective of castes. Religion cannot give any material benefit except mental satisfaction.

B. I have actively devoted some time and money for the propagation of the Dhamma. Now, I am doing nothing, due to personal bondage (problems).

4. *A lecturer of Commerce in a college, Age 35.*

A. *Though not economically, and socially, we mentally feel benefited as we are now linked with such a great religion of the universe.

B. One-fourth of my salary is being utilised for socio-religious work. And most of my time I am devoting for the propagation of the Dhamma.

5. *A well-to-do employee, a graduate; Age 34.*

A. *Not given economical advantage but we have been benefited mentally and psychologically.

B. I am not giving any time for the propagation of the Dhamma. But as far as money is concerned I contribute to the religious work without any hesitation.

6. *An employee of the Reserve Bank; triple post-graduate; Age 42.*

A. *There is no caste system in Buddhism; we ceased to belong to any caste, we are only Buddhists.

B. Whatever little time I get, I devote it for the propagation of the Dhamma. I am ever ready for discussion on Buddhism in comparison to other religions. I give a little money also for this purpose.

7. *A lady lecturer in a college teaching Marathi, Spinster, Age 30.*

A. *Yes, Neo-Buddhism has given benefit.

B. Very little time and money.

(She was the only lady, who responded to the questionnaire.)

8. *An electrical engineer, B.E., in Government service, Age 37.*

A. *I was benefited by comparing myself as equal as higher castes through the teaching of the Lord Buddha.

B. Whenever circumstances warrant, I do give my own time and money for the propagation of the Dhamma.

9. *A Government auditor; a double M.A., LL.B. and B.Ed; Age 50.*

A. *Yes, Neo-Buddhism has given benefit. This is under limitation, i.e., territorial or regional.

B. As per ability, i.e., by advising to create Vihar. In Vihar, on holidays, preaching and praying, so (that) the programme of get-together is advanced.

10. *An officer in the Reserve Bank; double M.A., BJ & LL.B; Age 40.*

A. *Yes, I feel no less than anybody else. It has given me psychological and material benefits.

B. I contribute subscriptions, donations, to various organisations who propagate the Dhamma; I contribute literature propagating it through various periodicals which are published by us as well as by other agencies.

11. *An officer in the Government; B.Sc. (Agri); Age 33.*

A. *Financial benefit, I got it. But the social benefit or advantage, I could not obtain.

B. Two hours daily in the evening are used to spend for the propagation of the Dhamma. Two per cent (2%) of my monthly income or more I spend for the Dhamma.

ANNEXURE III BUDDHIST POPULATION IN INDIA

The enumerated statistics of the population of India, systematically organised is available from 1881.The British Indian Empire comprised a vast territory, ranging from Middle East to Far East. Even after Indian Independence, (1947), princely States continued to exist till 1948 and the protuguese left the Indian soil only in the early sixties. Even the British Indian Territorial definition was changing every decade specially after the 1931 Census. Presenting massive Buddhist populace of the British Indian Empire at the close of the 19th century and the dawn of 20th century will be erroneous and misleading, and thus irrelevant. To add, the Re-organisation of States in 1956 makes it difficult to count the Buddhists statewise. Therefore, it is only after 1951 Census, we can note the Buddhist Statistics meaningfully and from 1961 effectively. Even then, the figures presented should be taken as minimum, because many practising Buddhists seem to have with held their identities as Buddhists due to various reasons or missed during the enumeration excercises. The Buddhist refugees from Tibet, when added, will swell the Indian Buddhist population further. It is difficult for those visitors, who had witnessed the multitude thronging 'Diksha Bhoomi' at Nagpur on the festivities of 14th October and 14th April, annually (coming from the length and breadth of India) to accept the low Buddhist population registered specially in Kerala, Tamil Nadu, Punjab and Haryana as correct.

The final analysis is as follows (as per census):

Year	*Total Buddhist Population in India*	*Percentage in India*
1961	3,200,333	.73%
1971	3,811,325	.70% of total population
1981	4,719,796	.71%

Census Figures—Buddhist Population in India

Sl.No.	*Name of the State*	*1951*	*1961*	*1971*	*1981*
1.	Andhra Pradesh	230	6753	10035	12930
2.	Assam	22628	36513	45212	NA
3.	Bihar	1092	2885	4806	3003
4.	Gujarat	198	3185	5469	7550
5.	Haryana	nil	736	845	761
6.	Himachal Pradesh	6308	18089	35937	52629
7.	Jammu & Kashmir	NA	48360	57956	69706
8.	Karnataka	1707	9770	14139	42147
9.	Kerala	90	228	605	223
10.	Madhya Pradesh	2291	113365	81823	75312
11.	Maharashtra	2487	2789501	3264223	3946149
12.	Manipur	33	325	495	473
13.	Meghalaya	nil	1011	1878	2739
14.	Nagaland	47	42	179	517
15.	Orissa	969	454	8462	8028
16.	Punjab	1660	2334	1374	799
17.	Rajasthan	4361	759	3642	4427
18.	Tamil Nadu	1179	777	1148	735
19.	Tripura	15203	33716	42285	54806
20.	Uttar Pradesh	3221	12893	39639	54542
21.	West Bengal	81665	112253	121504	156296

Special States/New States/Union Territories

		1951	*1961*	*1971*	*1981*
*	North East Frontier Agency	—	5809	—	—
*	Sikkim	39397	49894	—	—
*	Andaman & Nicobar Islands	1604	1707	103	—
*	Arunachal Pradesh	NA	NA	61400	86483
*	Chandigarh	nil	06	92	454
*	Dadra & Nagar Haveli	nil	02	73	189
*	Delhi	503	5466	8720	7117
*	Mizoram	—	—	—	40429
*	Pondicherry	NA	25	21	75
*	Lakshadweep Island	nil	nil	nil	nil

SELECT BIBLIOGRAPHY

Ahir, D.C., *Buddhism in Modern India*, Bhikku Nivas Prakasan, Nagpur, 1972, *Gandhi and Ambedkar*, Dr. Ambedkar Study Circle, Jalandhar, 1979, *How and Why Buddhism Declined in India*, Mahabodhi Society of India, New Delhi, 1978.

Amar Chitra Katha, Editor, *Baba Saheb Ambedkar*, India Book House (Education), Bombay, 1979.

Ambedkar, Dr. B.R., *Buddha and His Dhamma*, Siddharth College Publications, Bombay, 1957, *Buddha and Karl Marx*, M.D. Panchbai (Publisher), Nagpur, November 1964, *Castes in India*, Bheem Patrika Publications, Jalandhar, *The Rise and Fall of Hindu Women*, Bheem Patrika Publications, Jalandhar, 1977.

Ambedkar Lehar, (News Letter), London, October 14, 1978.

Baldwin, Robert E., *Economic Development and Growth*, John Wiley and Sons Inc., New York, 1966.

Bapat, Prof. P.V. (Ed.), *2500 Years of Buddhism*, Publications Division, Ministry of Information & Broadcasting, Govt. of India, New Delhi, 1971.

Bharathi, K.S., *Foundations of Ambedkar's Thought*, Dattsons, Nagpur, 1990.

Patrotic Call, Bodhisattvā Ambedkar's, The Buddhist Society of India, Hyderabad, 1978.

Nandi, Amar, *Constitution of India*, Bookland Private Limited, Calcutta, 1959.

Dalit Voice, Vol. II, No. 14, Bangalore, June 1-15, 1992.

Deep, Dr. Ambedkar, Study Circle, Nagpur, (Several Issues).

Dongre, Prof. M.K., *Economic Thoughts of Dr. Ambedkar*, Ambedkar Samaj Publications, Nagpur, 1974.

Edwards, Michael, *In the Blowing Out of a Flame*, George Allen & Urwin Ltd., London, 1976.

Giddens, Anthony, *Capitalism and Modern Social Theory—An Analysis of the Writings of Marx, Durkheim and Marx Weber*, Cambridge University Press, Cambridge, 1979, *Durkheim*, William Collins Sons & Co., Glassgow, 1978.

Kadam, K.N., *Ambedkar and the Significance of His Movement*, Popular Prakasan, Bombay, 1991.

Kuber, V.W., *B.R. Ambedkar*, Publications Division, Govt. of India, New Delhi, 1978.

Latourette, Kenneth, *Missions Tomorrow*, Harper and Brothers, New York, 1936.

MacMann. Lt. Gen. Sir John, *Religious and Hidden Cults of India*, Neeraj Publishing House, Delhi, 1982.

Nandasara, Ven. Pt. Hegoda, *Lectures Delivered in England*, Daya Henavitarse, London.

Nehru, Jawaharlal, *The Discovery of India*, The Signet Press, Calcutta, 1946.

Oldenberg, Hermann, *Buddha, His Doctrines, His Order*, India Book House, Delhi-Varanasi, 1971.

Pande, G.C., *Studies in the Origins of Buddhism*, University of Allahabad, Allahabad, 1957.

Pande, G.C. & Pande, P.C., *Social Anatomy of Economic Growth*, Anmol Publications, New Delhi, 1990.

Prabuddha Bharata, Vol. LXXXVIII, Mayavati, UP-Calcutta, November. 1978.

INDEX